UNLOCK THE AMERICAN DREAM

THE SECRETS OF STARTING YOUR OWN BUSINESS

DR. PAT LAINO ED.D, MS, CAS

outskirts
press

INTRODUCTION

My name is Dr. Pat Laino and all my friends and entrepreneur students call me Dr. Pat. I have written numerous workbooks over the past ten years and this one was finally completed and published.

This workbook is far different than most texts currently on the market about how to really start a business. I have taught and mentored hundreds of aspiring entrepreneurs who want to achieve the American Dream by successfully starting and operating profitable business ventures.

The American Dream is the belief that there are unlimited opportunities here in America where anyone can accomplish anything, if they work hard enough at it. This workbook is all about learning the most critical business skills and strategies to start-up your own business to achieve the American Dream. "Going from rags to riches" does and can happen here in our country because I'm a prime example. I started my business with "a dollar and a dream", worked extremely hard and now operate a highly successful six-figure business operation.

The American Dream was first coined by James T. Adams in 1931 during the "Great Depression". He described the American Dream as the complex social and political expectations found in our country. Adams stated that America has always been about liberty, rights, democracy and equality for all. These principles also include unlimited opportunities for prosperity and success that can be reached and this continues to be true today. The American Dream is all about being in a country of unlimited opportunities for all.

My mission here is to share with you what I faced in the "battle grounds" of starting my business and how I achieved and continue to live the American Dream. I have included conversations with some entrepreneurs as they too traveled the road to reaching the American Dream. There are also famous quotes to help spur you on.

In this work book you will learn, work on and master the following three specific stages to realize your American Dream:

Stage 1: Self Assessment to determine your entrepreneur expertise,
Stage 2: Research and create your own Business Action Plan and
Stage 3: Acquire the Business Skills to live the American Dream.

I recommend that you read this entire workbook to start your journey of reaching for the American Dream.

Table of Contents

STAGE ONE

———❧———

YOUR SELF ASSESSMENT

WHEN HOPEFUL ENTREPRENEURS come to me for training and coaching because they want to start a business, I start by discussing how they can reach for the American Dream by becoming a successful entrepreneur.

There is no better time than now to be an entrepreneur entering the world of business ownership because you will become part of the gigantic wave that's growing in size and sweeping across America. Numerous business researchers predict that in the future most major innovations and changes throughout the world will come from entrepreneurs like you and me.

Initially, you will assess the pros and cons of starting your own business because this is the first test to determine if a business undertaking is for you. I've discovered through the years that successful entrepreneurs are never ordinary people. They are extraordinary individuals with a vision. They stay extremely focused all the while they are starting and operating their business.

The real value of this workbook lies in teaching you the specific life and business skills needed to reach the American Dream. Starting your business is perhaps the most important step that you will ever take in your life, so you better get it "right" the first time.

**Famous Quote: Logic will get you from A to B. Imagination will take you everywhere
(Albert Einstein, Scientist, 1879-1955).**

Using specific entrepreneur skills is what makes the difference between business malfunction and your success. Each of us has some skills to pursue the American Dream and if you don't have some of the following skills, now is the time to acquire these.

AN EYE FOR OPPORTUNITY:

Successful entrepreneurs tend to see opportunities that others don't. When going into your business, begin by finding a unique need and let nothing stand in your way of satisfying it.

AN APPETITE FOR HARD WORK AIMED AT MAKING MONEY:

Focusing on "real" money-making work is what successful entrepreneurs do best. They know that it's difficult at first, chaotic in the middle and terrific in the end.

Famous Quote: Work is love made visible
(Kahlil Gibran, Prophet and Philosopher, 1883-1931).

PROBLEM SOLVER:

They see problems as challenges and when these are solved they are ecstatic.

Famous Quote: We read the world wrong and say that it deceives us
(Rabindranth Tagore, Author, 1861-1941).

DELEGATES:

Successful entrepreneurs never do anything someone can do for them because this permits them to stay on target to meet their busy schedule.

DISCIPLINE:

It's not how hard you work but rather the way you work that truly counts. The thriving entrepreneur resists the temptation to do what comes easy, instead of what's really essential to making money.

SELF CONFIDENCE & ADAPTABILITY:

Winning entrepreneurs are extremely self-confident and accept risks as opportunities. They think that the greater the risk, the greater the reward.

Famous Quote: It takes courage to grow up and turn out to be who you really are
(E.E. Cummings, Dramatist, 1894-1962).

ABILITY TO MANAGE MY TIME:

"Time is money" and they use it wisely by prioritizing.

Famous Quote: Your time is limited; don't waste it living someone else's life
(Steve Jobs, American Inventor, 1955-2011).

ABILITY TO HANDLE STRESS:

Managing stress is the skill of winners because they know how to make stress work for them in stressful situations.

DESIRE TO SUCCEED:

Successful entrepreneurs have a single-minded, almost compulsive desire to achieve the American Dream.

ENTREPRENEUR QUESTIONNAIRE

1. Why do I want to go into my own business?

   _____

   _____

2. How strong is my desire to succeed in business? (describe your feelings)

   _____

   _____

3. What unique product or service will I offer?

   _____

   _____

4. How do I know that there are enough customers to generate ample profits?

   _____

   _____

5. What makes my business unique and different from my competitors?

   _____

   _____

6. How will my business image radiate my success?

   _____

   _____

7. What management skills do I have to effectively operate this business?

   _____

   _____

8. Here are two examples of my "pushing on" when the going gets tough.

   _____

   _____

STRENGTHS

What makes me think that I can start my own business and achieve the American Dream?

WEAKNESSES

Who are my competitors and what are they doing better than me?

**Famous Quote: Everything you ever wanted is on the other side of fear
(George W. Adair, Icon Real Estate Developer, 1823-1899).**

OPPORTUNITIES

What makes my business unique, cost-effective and ensures that I will have sufficient customers to generate a profit?

THREATS

What are the threats that could impact my success and how will I handle these?

Dr. Pat's Inside Secret:
I became very proactive while identifying my SWOT responses because
I knew that "failure was not an option".

STRENGTHS:

- More than half of my potential customers are very affluent
- My financial position and credit rating are excellent
- The local Bank is already considering my loan
- I have the experience and expertise to start-up my company

OPPORTUNITIES:

- Research shows that there are sufficient customers
- Our suppliers have offered to share their bill boards at no cost
- There are additional potential customers in adjacent areas
- My major competitor is retiring

WEAKNESSES

- There are two competitors that appear to be slowing down
- Some price-conscious customers have already been identified
- There is a potential recession in a related field
- Personnel will require costly training

THREATS

- A new competitor has recently been identified
- Cost of our raw materials is rising
- The local Census show a slight decrease in the population

PROS & CONS OF GOING INTO BUSINESS:

This is an exercise to make you aware of the benefits and pitfalls of going into your own business. In the final analysis, the pros should outweigh the cons for you to really start up your business.

**Famous Quote: Don't' let the noise of other's opinion drown your inner voice
(Steve Jobs, American Icon & Inventor, 1955-2011).**

PROS   CONS

REACHING FOR THE AMERICAN DREAM:

Strong leadership skills were essential while I was striving to reach the American Dream. The definition of a leader is: "an action person who directs, commands, guides, conducts and performs" (Webster's Dictionary).

To reach the American Dream, the following skills kept me focused:

- Always set specific goals with a focus on achieving these
- I'm persistent and let nothing stand in my way
- Hard work is my passion
- I'm a visionary and a creative thinker
- Problems are opportunities to be solved
- I'm a leader in the business arena
- Managing my time and stress are what I do well
- Coordinating my family and business is a major priority
- Conflict management is my expertise
- I recognize opportunities to make money to show growth
- Market analyzer is my name and this what I do best
- People call me the networking genius

Famous Quote: There is no secret to success. It's the result of preparation, hard work and learning from failure (Colin Powell, American Four Star General, 1937 to present).

Successful owners stay focused on the following three most important business-related assumptions to attain their American Dream:

- *Money*: **Awareness of available capital at all times**
- *Materials*: **Knowledge of your physical properties**
- *People*: **Responsible for all those who impact operations**

Famous Quote: It is not what we take up, but what we give up, that makes us rich (Henry Ward Beecher, American Clergy and Social Reformer 1813-1887).

OBSTACLES THAT GET IN THE WAY OF THE AMERICAN DREAM

It's always wise to be aware of what obstacles that can get in your way while you're reaching for the American Dream. Here are some of my obstacles that I encountered and conquered:

Famous Quote: Take the fist step in faith. You don't have to see the whole staircase, just take the fist step (Martin Luther King, Famous Clergy, 1929-1968).

1. Lack of a written Business Action Plan
Initially, I said that my Plan was all in my head, but it didn't' take me long to discover that I needed a written Plan if I wanted to succeed.

2. Going it alone

In the beginning, I was able to function alone, but as the business started to grow, I needed to hire employees including: the technician who assumed some of my work load, a manager to run the overall operations, the financial manager and I continued as the visionary.

3. Run out of cash

In the excitement of starting my business, I lost sight of the actual amount of money that I needed to operate during my first year. I took my Business Action Plan to the bank and secured a micro-loan.

4. Not knowing my customers' specific wants and needs

I discovered that if I did not stay abreast with my customers' emerging wants and needs, then I knew that I was heading for failure.

5. Ignoring the numbers

I made a bold statement that I was in business to make a profit and that was my "bottom line". I quickly hired a reliable bookkeeper to monitor and report to me about my ongoing financial status.

6. Its human nature to be attracted to what's popular or hot

I was very careful that I chose a business operation that didn't have the potential of "fizzling out" fast. I stayed current with what was going on in my business world and stayed alert for trends that come and go. I had to be constantly aware of what my customers wanted and were willing to continue to pay.

STAGE TWO

———— ❧ ————

BUSINESS ACTION PLAN

OVER THE PAST two decades, I have instructed and coached hundreds of hopeful entrepreneurs, who participated in a six-month small business training program, developed their own Plan and many are now living the American Dream.

Dr. Pat's Inside Secret:
The first thing that I say to all of my aspiring entrepreneurs is to "Go for the American Dream".
Remember when you were a young child and your parents said that you could do anything.
To succeed, you must revert back to the times when anything was possible and everything is possible here in this country.

You've completed the inventory of your strengths and weaknesses in stage one and have now decided to develop your very own individualized Business Action Plan (Plan).

Famous Quote: How wonderful it is that nobody need wait a single moment before starting to improve the world
(Anne Frank, Jewish Author and Victim of the Holocaust, 1929-1945).

You may be thinking, "Why should I take the time to create my Plan?

This Plan is your exclusive personal and business profile that will lead you to reaching the American Dream. It's the official document to take to your lender or anyone else who may need to know about your operations.

Let me state upfront that you have very little chance of securing a business loan unless you have a detailed Plan to take to your financial institution for the loan officer to review.

When others read your Plan it will give them an overview of your anticipated business venture and it adds credibility on whether or not your venture will be successful. This Plan is also your written communications tool when you need to orient others such as an attorney, financial advisor, employees, sales personnel or your suppliers.

Lenders will want some type of collateral to ensure that you are serious about starting your business. The most common collateral is some of your savings or other assets and we will discuss loan rationale later on. A word of warning; I have met with entrepreneurs in the past who want to put their home up for collateral to guarantee their loan. This is a very serious choice because you certainly don't want to jeopardize losing your home if your business encounters trouble.

Conversations with an entrepreneur winner: I started by getting rid of my former poor employer, former negative friends and anything "former" that dragged me down. I learned from the past, buried it and moved on.

Your individualized Plan must ensure that your focus is aimed at making money. This planning tool should evolve into your "road map" to success. It will add stability and help ensure your good name and a high level of profitability.

Conversations with an entrepreneur winner: I started my Business Plan by telling myself over and over again that I was going to make money. I walk, talk and dress the part of success with this "aura" all of the time and yes, I'm now very successful!

The benefit of your Plan is that it can take you "over the top" when reaching for the American Dream. It makes it easier to inform everyone about what business you are opening. Your Plan is the path in seeking the American Dream because it guides you through the turbulent economic seas and into a "harbor of choice".

Conversations with an entrepreneur winner: One creative entrepreneur told me that she imaged herself as a fine race horse, with the main focus on winning the race. By the way, she opened a successful horse farm where she teaches her customers how to ride and care for horses.

THE VISION OF MY AMERICAN DREAM:

Before you start to work on your Plan, sit down in a quiet place for at least a couple of hours when no one else is around and envision what achieving the American Dream will mean to you.

The successful owner that you want to become should dream like Ray Kroc, the founder of McDonalds, who envisioned a structured food operation that could be replicated everywhere. With very little money, he dreamed of growing his vision by staying focused. Today there are thousands of McDonald franchise owners worldwide and 95% of them are achieving the American Dream. Now ask yourself, why do 88% of all small businesses fail when 35,000 McDonald's are successful today? Why can't your business be a winner too?

Famous Quote: There isn't a person anywhere who isn't capable of doing more than they think they can (Henry Ford, Founder of Ford Motor Company, 1863-1947).

Make a copy of this page and begin to create your future vision of how you see your business operation in five years. Forget the negative and dream the positive about your American Dream.

Right from the very start of your planning, envision your business as the greatest, before this even happens. Think and act big and tell yourself that the morale is high among the employees and there is energy and excitement everywhere. Walk, talk and dress the part of the greatest business owner of all times.

Famous Quote: You must do the thing you think you can not do
(Eleanor Roosevelt, First Lady, American Diplomat, 1884-1962).

Here's a sample of my American Dream after five years in operation:

- My business is a streamline operation where everything depicts order and success far beyond any of my expectations
- Plenty of customers are coming and going
- The huge parking lot is full of my customers' cars
- My twenty great employees are happy and busy
- Expansion activities are underway at this location
- I'm adding new products/services that have tested positive
- My business loan is paid off
- I have no outstanding debt at this time
- Voted #1 Business of the Year by my colleagues
- This business effectively operates when I'm not here everyday
- Customers, employees, family and the business world know that I have successfully accomplished the American Dream.

Place your written vision in a safe place and look at your responses every month and especially when you think the "going gets tough". It may take you five years and sixty reviews, but I'm sure that you will be well on your way toward the American Dream.

Conversations with numerous entrepreneur winners: They say that their work and play overlap so much that they don't know if they are working or playing because they enjoy both of these so much.

The thriving business owners of the world commonly demonstrate drive, dedication, persistence, diligence and a no-fail entrepreneurial attitude. They are eager to try out new ideas, while putting their life on fast forward and eagerly look for their "next mountain to climb".

The common traits of less-than-successful entrepreneurs that I have seen throughout the past twenty years are that they are unable to stay focused long enough to do any planning. They say that their Plan is all in their head and this makes bank financing impossible. Stress is an everyday occurrence, along with a life full of drama, struggles and chaos. They fail to have a vision and they lack the Plan that could take them there.

HOW I WILL REACH THE AMERICAN DREAM:
THIS IS THE VISION OF MY BUSINESS IN FIVE YEARS:

POINT 1: EXECUTIVE SUMMARY

This is the first point that you will include in your Business Action Plan (Plan). Initially, you will start working on this, but it will not be fully completed until all of the other points in your Plan are finished.

The Executive Summary should be finalized last! This point gives a clear overview of your business operation to the readers. It should be no longer than two pages and represent a concise, clear and broad narrative about your business operation.

I made my Executive Summary professional, concise and I was enthusiastic in the manner in which I presented the contents. My entire summary was checked over and over for spelling and format.

I started with a brief mission statement featuring what the positive fundamentals of my operations were and why I thought this business venture would be successful and profitable.

Creating this statement requires a great deal of time to make it as powerful as possible to bring about the results that you hope for. I also confirmed that I had researched my specific product and service lines, found a suitable site, located sufficient customers and structured my pricing to realize a profit. I concluded that I will implement effective marketing and advertisement strategies and hire experienced personnel.

Conversations with an entrepreneur winner: I keep my business operations simple and play by the basic rule that more money has to come in than goes out. I talk to my financial manager everyday.

HOW I WILL REACH THE AMERICAN DREAM:
THIS IS WHAT I WILL INCLUDE IN MY EXECUTIVE SUMMARY:

POINT 2: PURPOSE & LEGAL STATUS

Many business owners go broke simply because they are confused about what the exact legal structure of their operations should be. Denoting your legal status is an important issue that needs to be addressed and included in your Plan.

When I started my business, I researched legal issues such as:

- Licensing and bonding requirements
- Permits local and state
- Health, workplace or environmental regulations
- Special regulations covering your industry or profession
- Zoning or building code requirements
- Insurance coverage
- Trade marks, copyrights and/or patents

Dr. Pat's Inside Secret:
Never sign a legal document unless your attorney reviews it and agrees to its contents.

Here is additional information that I explored before opening my own business:

SOLE PROPRIETORSHIP:

The sole proprietorship legal form is the easiest method that many new start up businesses use. You need to go to the clerk's office in your county and file a "Doing Business As" (DBA) for a nominal fee. This clerk will research whether or not anyone in this country is using your business name, if so, then a new business name needs to be selected.

Sole proprietor means that you are the sole owner of this business. You will be personally responsible and liable for all of the business debts. The disadvantage of a sole proprietorship is that if you die, then the business dies with you.

PARTNERSHIP:

This legal form should never be considered without the advice and guidance of your attorney. The reason is that if one partner leaves town, the other is responsible for all of the business debts. If a partner accrues debts on a business credit card, then all partners are liable for these debts.

Conversations with an entrepreneur winner: If you are going to have a partner, do not use their attorney, even if it's free. Your partner's attorney is not going to watch out for your welfare, so secure your own attorney.

In any legal action, all partners will be sued personally with property, bank accounts and more being attached. A marriage is easier to get out of than a partnership! Very few survive the breakup of a business partnership without the business collapsing.

Dr. Pat's Inside Secret:
Before you take a partner, I suggest that you ask yourself; "Why do I need a partner?" If it's money, then go to a loan officer. If it's for management needs, then hire a manager. Think about what a partner will do for you, not what you can do for them and seek the advice of your attorney.

CORPORATION (INC.) AND LIMITED LIABILITY CORPORATION (LLC):

The Corporation and the Limited Liability Corporation exist as separate entities and one of these legal forms may be the best way for you to start your business. This is dependent on your attorney's advice.

In the form of a corporation, you will be personally protected by the "corporate shield", unless you are grossly negligent or there is fraud involved. Lending institutions are more likely to fund a corporation than a sole proprietor, according to my attorney.

The major disadvantage is the prospect of double taxation because the corporation must pay taxes on its net income and then you must pay taxes on your wages and on any dividends.

Some other disadvantages are stricter laws concerning the operations of your business, additional detailed accounting procedures and massive paperwork. This results in much higher operational costs with this legal form.

Conversations with an entrepreneur winner: I found that attorney fees vary and the incorporation paper work was going to be very costly, so I researched and found an attorney whose costs were the most reasonable for a job well done.

LIMITED PARTNERSHIP:

This is much like a corporation and the costs are comparable. This occurs when outside investors become limited partners with you. They are only personally liable for the amount of their investment and that is all that this investor can lose. The question here is whether all limited partnerships are just that, and for tax purposes these are questionable. Some businesses may be taxed as a partnership and others as a corporation. It's all at the determination of the IRS, so check with your attorney on this form of partnership.

Summary: All of these legal forms may change with time; new forms come in and previous forms go out. This is why you must turn to your attorney for advice and guidance about what legal form is best for your business operation. Never assume that you can operate without their professional assistance because paying their fees upfront is much better that paying later on for the trouble that can evolve without this legal advice.

HOW I WILL REACH THE AMERICAN DREAM:
HOW DO I DETERMINE WHAT LEGAL STATUS MY BUSINESS WILL ASSUME?

The definition of a leader is "An action person who directs, commands, guides, conducts and performs" (Webster's Dictionary). Once an owner sees that the business is starting to grow because their products or services are in great demand then this is the time the owner should be astute enough to hire employees.

To achieve the American Dream, successful entrepreneurs need to demonstrate and apply strong leadership skills that let them thrive in the business arena.

**Famous Quote: Change your thoughts and you change your world
(Norman Vincent Peale, Motivational Speaker, 1898-1993).**

Numerous businesses start-up when a person decides to open their own business because they have the technical skills and they want to become their own boss. I have seen many businesses fail because the owner assumes the responsibility of running the entire business, void of anyone else. They focus only on the technical services that they know best and everything else falls by the wayside.

**Dr. Pat's Inside Secret:
All business structures should include the entrepreneur who has the ideas, the technician who knows how to produce the service or product, the business manager who oversee the operations and the financial manager who handles and monitors the finances.**

The key question to address here in your Plan is who will successfully bring about an acceptable level of profitability for this business? You need to respond to what you will do when your company starts growing. A case must be built that there will be a strong management team ready to handle the growth period.

Before I even began to operate my business, I identified my banker, accountant and attorney and how each one of them would function in my operations. I included their names, addresses, emails, telephone numbers and their key role in my Plan.

HOW I WILL REACH THE AMERICAN DREAM:
**THIS IS HOW I WILL SET UP AND OPERATE MY COMPANY WHILE KEEPING
A FOCUS ON GROWTH:**

The right employees and staff are vital to the success of all businesses and they must know their job duties and responsibilities to be effective. All of my current employees have been with me since the start of my business twenty years ago. I added new employees as my business grew. I don't tell them what to do, only what has to be done.

Their job descriptions are precise and reviewed every December or more often if their workload changes. This keeps everyone happy and doing what they are suppose to do to get their job done.

Famous Quote: You should always ask yourself what would happen if everyone did what you were doing (Jean-Paul Sarte, Philosopher and Author, 1905-1980).

Before you even consider hiring anyone, develop a job description for each employee and a time for employee evaluation.

Conversations with an entrepreneur winner: I started my business by developing job descriptions for every employee, including myself. I did not want to be running around trying to get jobs done, while my employees were trying to find jobs to do.

Sometimes in the early stages of a business you may want to hire temporary help or consider leasing employees when needed, but remember that they will frequently have less of a commitment to your company. Be certain that their background checks are available to you before they start.

Dr. Pat's Inside Secret:
I recommend that you start out your search for employees by creating an application form that specifically targets the type of employee that you want to hire to do a specific job. You can go online and find a generic job application form and then tailor it to meet your needs.

Studies show that employees are one of the main reasons why customers stop coming to a place of business or stop buying a product or service. It's usually because of the lack of prompt and courteous attention. As an astute owner you need to regularly observe how your employees treat customers.

Famous Quote: If you hire people just because they can do the job, they will work for your money. If you hire people who believe what you believe, they'll work for you with blood, sweat and tears (Simon Sinek, American Author, 1941 to present).

Dr. Pat's Inside Secret:
As an added safety measure, I conduct background checks before I hire any employee.

When commencing my business, I researched, recorded and retained data about my potential employees, calculated how many I needed, the type of labor required (skilled, unskilled or professionals), job descriptions, background checks and the pay structure. In addition an employee evaluation system, termination rules, the non-compete and confidentiality forms were developed.

Another item to address in your Plan is that if you are going to be the only worker at the onset of your business then what happens to your operations if you become ill or incapacitated. You need to identify a person with the experience and expertise to ensure that the business operations will run smoothly without major problems. This information is extremely important if you are seeking bank financing because the loan officer has to be certain that there is someone to effectively carry on your operations so that the loan can be repaid.

HOW I WILL ACHIEVE THE AMERICAN DREAM
WHAT IS THE LINK BETWEEN EMPLOYEES AND MY ACHIEVING THE AMERICAN DREAM?

HOW WILL I BE CERTAIN THAT MY EMPLOYEES ARE DOING THEIR JOB?

POINT 5: PRODUCT OR SERVICE DESCRIPTION

Famous Quote: "Find a need and satisfy it" are the words of Aristotle Onassis (Famous Shipping Magnate, 1906-1975). He went from "rages to riches" to bring about his overwhelming business success. In later life he married Jackie Kennedy, former First Lady.

There must be sufficient customers willing to pay what you're charging and the results have to produce a healthy profit margin. One thing you should seriously consider is whether or not various changes can impact your operations such as closure of your road for repairs or winter storms.

In this point of your Plan you will need to clearly describe what your products or services are and emphasize why customer will buy from you and not your competitors. Describe your products or services in detail, highlight their uniqueness and compare your prices to those of your competitors.

My own Plan clearly specified my services that were not currently found in the market place. My prices were more reasonable than my competitors and my site was convenient, safe and handicapped accessible site, with a great deal of parking.

Dr. Pat's Inside Secret:

I added this statement in my Plan: "We do expect competitors to increase, but we will address these challenges by hiring additional and well-trained employees to serve our customers".

HOW I WILL ACHIEVE THE AMERICAN DREAM

THESE ARE THE REASONS WHY CUSTOMERS WILL BUY MY PRODUCT OR SERVICE OVER MY COMPETITORS:

POINT 6: CUSTOMER PROFILE

Identifying and reaching your customers is what will put you in the American Dream arena.

Dr. Pat's Inside Secret:

Customers are made of gold and if you have them then you have a goldmine.

This is the point in your Plan where you include all of the data about your customers:

Age Bracket: **Sex:**

_____   _____

Average Income: _____

Where do they live? _____

What is their life style (married, single, family, sport-minded etc.)

_____

What outside events could impact the buying power of your potential customers?

_____

_____

What other reasons could influence your customers to buy your product or services

_____

_____

HOW WILL I ACHIEVE THE AMERICAN DREAM
WHAT MUST I KNOW ABOUT MY CUSTOMERS THAT WILL IMPACT MY REACHING THE AMERICAN DREAM?

HOW WILL I KNOW HOW EMPLOYEES ARE TREATING CUSTOMERS?

WHAT WILL BE DONE TO HANDLE A CUSTOMER COMPLAINT?

POINT 7: LOCATION

Location is one of the most important elements to achieving the American Dream and must be fully explained in your Plan.

Conrad Hilton, founder of the famous Hilton Hotel chain (1887-1979) was asked what made his business a success and he replied; "location, location, location".

Dr. Pat's Inside Secret:
I have seen numerous companies that have the best products on the market but they still fail. It is because of poor locations or unsafe neighborhoods. Customers did not patronize these stores no matter how much they advertised. They went out of business but could have been successful if they had the right location. In addition, be certain that you have the zoning in place to operate a business at your site.

When I was ready to open my current business, I explored numerous sites that could be leased or purchased. I finally signed a three year lease after my attorney reviewed it and agreed on the terms.

The following data was included in my Plan: this site was in an ideal busy, downtown location at a very reasonable monthly cost and priced lower than any other acceptable site. The owner will do all of the renovations at no cost. It had equipment which was state-of-the-art and conference rooms that we could use without charge.

The location was very safe, handicapped accessible, plenty of free parking, ample space for my staff and enough storage space. Signage could be seen by hundreds of cars that passed here everyday. Our customers could easily reach our downtown site by car, plane, bus or train.

HOW WILL I ACHIEVE THE AMERICAN DREAM
WHY IS THE LOCATION SO IMPORTANT TO MY BUSINESS SUCCESS?

POINT 8: PRICING

One of the most difficult challenges for me when starting my business was how to determine the selling price of my products and services that would result in an acceptable profit level.

I remember one entrepreneur who came in seeking assistance because she couldn't meet her overhead expenses and wanted help in seeking a loan. She lacked a Plan and agreed to start working on one immediately. When I asked if she had customers, she replied: "More than I can handle". This was a red flag because if you have sufficient customers and you're charging enough, then you ought to be able to pay your bills and generate profits.

She created floral arrangement primarily for weddings and funerals. She didn't know who her competitors were, much less what they charged. This story does have a happy ending because she went on to complete her Plan and learned how to calculate the price of every arrangement that made her a healthy profit. Within seven months, she was able to cover her overhead expenses, had no need for a loan and actually drew a sufficient salary.

The misconception is that we must sell cheap to keep our customers and this is not so. Instead of putting this misconception in the forefront, change your way of thinking and cost out either a single product or service. This point in your Plan must clearly show that you know how to determine a price to make a profit.

Conversations with an entrepreneur winner: One of my graduates who opened his business said; "I found a product that my customers can't live without and this is the secret to my success". I measure my ongoing success by the high level of my healthy profits.

There are four basic elements to consider when calculating a price to charge. These are: cost of materials/supplies, hourly wages to make the product or to perform the service, packaging/handling costs and some money for overhead.

To determine a selling price, no matter what method you use, you need to end up with an acceptable profit margin. You may find it easier to calculate what you will charge when you first start out by using one of the following methods.

An example of costing out a product:

1. It cost $5 for material = $5

2. It takes one hour to make the final product $ 10

3. Packaging & handling costs $ 2

4. Add 1, 2, 3, x this by 2 to cover some over head costs and the selling price is $34

An example of costing out a service:

Those who perform a job tend to charge hourly or a flat fee.

1. It cost $5 for supplies to use = $ 5

2. It takes 4 hours to do the job and 1 hour travel time = $ 50

3. Add 1, 2, x this by 2 to cover some over head costs and the selling price is $110

Until your book keeper and financial advisor develop a more precise costing-out strategy, you can use one of these methods. Check to see what your competitors are charging to decide if you can afford to make your product or render your service. If you can't make a profit, then go back to the drawing board and immediately reconsider your business venture.

Another area to research is whether or not to sell on credit and wait for your customers to pay. Determine if it's customary to extend credit in your field of business. The questions are: How will you check the customer's creditworthiness and what happens if they don't pay? In addition, what will it cost you in lost profits to extend credit?

Conversations with an entrepreneur winner: Goldie always wanted to open a store and sell hand-made jewelry, but when she computed her over-head and production costs, she could not afford to open a store front. Instead, she started selling online that resulted in making a very healthy profit.

HOW I WILL ACHIEVE THE AMERICAN DREAM
WHY IS PRICING SO IMPORTANT IN REACHING FOR THE AMERICAN DREAM?

It's very important to address this point in your Plan because you must "get the word" out there to attract enough customers to produce a healthy profit level.

There is a distinct difference between marketing and advertisement:

Marketing is **<u>identifying</u>** who your customers are and
Advertisement is **<u>reaching</u>** these customers.

No matter how good your products or services are, your business venture cannot succeed without effective marketing to identify and reach your customers. This begins with targeted research to make certain that you are on the right track. You need to research who your customers really are and where they are located.

Your Plan should include all of your marketing and advertisement strategies that will bring your product or service to the forefront over your competitors. If you fail to do this, then you will fall short of attracting your customers.

SOCIAL MEDIA MARKETING:

The buzz around social media marketing has been growing to a near climax. Business operators have been getting into the action by discovering powerful new tools for engaging customers online. By combining social media with email marketing, business owners have found yet another way to stay on top of their market and become well connected with their target audience.

Social media marketing allows you to engage with your social network using relevant and effective content. As people interact and you share your business-related content, it creates a word-of-mouth effect allowing you to reach additional customers and drive more business to you.

There is a great deal to consider in the social media arena. It's vital that you are aware of and keep up with Facebook, Twitter, email and whatever new social network that may be emerging.

Some of the most current social media networks at a glance are:

FACEBOOK: Currently, this is the largest social media site. It allows you to easily create profiles, connect with your customers and others to share photos and videos.

TWITTER: This let's you send and read short messages called "tweets". You can follow anyone from customers to companies.

LINKEDIN: Designed specifically for the business community. It allows its members to establish networks of people they know and trust to link with their contacts' network.

PINTEREST: This is a virtual "Bulletin Board" that allows users to upload, save, sort and Pin images and other media content.

INSTAGRAM: This is a popular platform focusing predominately on sharing photos.

GOOGLE PLUS: This allows users a more diverse social media experience including; Facebook-like posting and multi-person video chats and more.

Many business owners are skeptical to try using social media. Here are a few of the excuses used by some of my entrepreneurs: I'm too busy, don't know where to start, don't know what site is right for my business and I don't have the time or help to keep my site updated and looking good.

You can't afford to allow your business to stay on the social media sidelines. You need to get into the "game" by becoming involved with the most notable social media marketing sites. If you lack the skills to develop and set up your own site, then seek the assistance of an expert. Obtain three quotes from social media site developers and then determine the most cost-effective one to use.

ADVERTISEMENT

My questions about advertisement are: how do I reach my customers, what media do I use and how do I measure the outcomes.

Paid advertisement may include my social media presence, newspaper ads, TV commercials and bill boards.

Free advertisement may include the initial announcement of your business start-up by the news media; free Informational Seminars, and participating in networking events. Impressive signage, your logo and business cards are also very effective and long-lasting advertisement tools.

ADDITIONAL OUTREACH STRATEGIES:

Check all the ways that you plan on selling your products/services:

Web Site __	**Telephone Sales**__	**Billboards**__	**A Catalog**__
Flea Markets__	**By Appointment**__	**Direct Mailings**__	**TV Ads**__
Newspaper Ads__	**Street Vendors**__	**Consignment**__	**Radio**__
Internet Sales__	**At other Locations** __	**Cold Calls**__	

METHODS TO COST OUT ADVERTISEMENT:

Once I identified my customer base, the next step was to review the four basic methods of allocating my advertisement dollars:

Method 1: Use a percentage of sales or profits:

If you select this method, then you will set aside 2% to 4% of your sales for advertisement. Question is; what happens when sales decline and this is the time when you need more advertisement, not less. Explain why you would use this method.

Method 2: Unit of sales:

You can set aside a fixed amount for each unit of sales, based upon your experience of how much advertising it takes to sell a unit. If you select this method, explain the rationale.

Method 3: Objective and task:

This method is seldom used because it appears complicated. It can be made easier if you identify specific ways to increase sales and then start! Take one specific strategy to increase sales, identify which media vehicle you'll use and then estimate the cost. Repeat this method for each product/service and measure the outcomes.

Method 4: Setting aside a specific dollar amount:

This method is often used by the novice entrepreneur. A dollar amount is set aside for advertisement costs, with no rationale for why that specific amount was selected.

Dr. Pat's Inside Secret:

Networking is one of the best-kept secrets that I could share with you. This is one of the most effective methods to market, advertise and promote you and your business. It's the true art of communication, when you will meet new business contacts, customers and friends that you haven't met before. Seek out opportunities to meet others who may help to open new doors and add to your achieving success.

HOW I WILL ACHIEVE THE AMERICAN DREAM
How will I use Social Media Marketing?

What other specific strategies will I use to achieve my American Dream?

POINT 10: COMPETITORS

All businesses have competitors and your Plan should reflect that you are fully aware of who they are. You need to list their location, prices, strengths and weakness. Let the readers of your Plan know why your products or services are a better buy and what makes yours unique.

Famous Quote: Forgive your enemies, but never forget their names (John F Kennedy, 35th US President, 1917-1963).

When I first started my business, I researched my competitors by analyzing all the data that I could find such as trade magazines, their online data and scanning newspapers for their ads.

I recommend that you research at least three of your competitors or other business sites to observe and gather data to add to your Plan:

Name of Business:

Address:

City & State

Email Address: **Telephone #:**

Your impression of their site:

Employees: their attitude and expertise:

Image of products or services:

Pricing structure:

The overall strengths & weaknesses of this competitor:

To further my research about competitors, I make onsite visits to many businesses similar to mine. When I was there, I came to the conclusions about what I could replicate to improve my business. The following observations were made and analyzed:

EXTERIOR OBSERVATIONS:

Signage: Visibility, size and colors
Windows: Attractive or not, cleanliness and/or limitations
Location: Ample parking, safe, easy access and handicapped spaces

INTERIOR OBSERVATIONS:

Employees ready to greet and help you
Initial greeting: Warm, cold, happy or no greeting at all
Lighting: Bright, cheerful or dismal
Displays: Messy, neat and orderly
Pricing: Appears high, low or just right
Let the readers of your Plan know that you are fully aware of your competition.

Conversations with an entrepreneur winner: I look at the world with a sense of wonderment and visualize what it will take to create something new like a product not yet found in the market place.

HOW I WILL ACHIEVE THE AMERICAN DREAM
WHY IS LEARNING ABOUT THE SUCCESS OF MY COMPETITORS SO IMPORTANT TO MY ATTAINING THE AMERICAN DREAM?

POINT 11: RESEARCH & DEVELOPMENT

In this point, you need to continuously spend time thoroughly researching your product or service.

Conversations with an entrepreneur winner: I never stop researching and learning because success comes by staying alert in the life-long information arena since business throughout the world has gotten so competitive.

I added in my Plan that a great deal of time was spent researching my service and product lines. I implemented a structured process of researching and identifying what my customers wanted and needed. Using this information, I then created the most efficient and cost effective strategies to achieve the desired results of making a profit.

My Plan also confirmed that I have been researching several potential sources of new services that will help to retain prior customers and attract new ones. I stated that I would focus on serving my customers well so that they will continue to come back.

Dr. Pat's Inside Secret:
I start all of my research strategies by thinking "outside of the box" about what new service I could add that would bring in more customers and money. I visualized the profits before I even start the race.

HOW I WILL ACHIEVE THE AMERICAN DREAM
WHY IS IT IMPORTANT TO CONTINUE TO CONDUCT RESEARCH IN MY FIELD OF BUSINESS OPERATIONS?

THESE ARE THREE SOURCES OF RESEARCH AIMED AT MY ACHIEVING THE AMERICAN DREAM:

POINT 12: TARGETING NEW MARKETS

I included in my Plan that I conducted extensive and targeted research to clearly support that my business venture would be viable and a profit could be realized. Whoever reads my Plan must be made aware that I have done my "homework" and there is a target market for my product or service when sold at a reasonable price.

To continue my company's growth, I immediately started to explore new market places so that I would be prepared for the growth that I expected to achieve in the future.

Famous Quote: An innovator is one who does not know it cannot be done
(R.A. Mashelkar, Scientist and Fellow of the Royal Society, 1943 to present).

I began forecasting early on about how I could enter into potential new and emerging markets. This time-sensitive preparation included moving into these new regions very soon.

My ongoing plans included staying alert to the possibilities of new profit-generating expansions, participating in the Trade Association related to my line of business to stay alert about possible changes in my industry, continuous networking and securing new customers, products and services.

Conversations with as entrepreneur winner: Before I started my business I anticipated that something might go wrong and I had better be able to think fast on my feet by being proactive rather than reactive. These were my first newly-acquired skills of pre-planning for the unexpected.

HOW I WILL ACHIEVE THE AMERICAN DREAM
How can I stay alert about what could impact business?

POINT 13: INITIAL START-UP COSTS

In this point you will need to address the specific costs associated with effectively starting your business. Frequently, a new owner will have some existing equipment, furniture or office supplies that they will be using. These should be listed as your assets. What you have are assets and what you need will be listed under expenses.

This is very important because when you list existing inventory or equipment the loan officer views these assets as a plus when you are requesting your loan. Next, list all of the office needs, equipment, inventory and anything else that you don't have but need to start your business operation.

List what you will need to set up your office such as desks, chairs, lamps, file cabinets, computer (hardware and software), printer, telephone, FAX machine and anything else that comprises your office set up. List a price for each item and if it's over $500 then I suggest that you get three estimates and add the rationale for your selection.

Next, you will itemize what you need in equipment. Will you buy or lease and explain the justification. It is wise to obtain three bids for each major piece of equipment and do a comparison of prices for the best deal.

Inventory that you need should be identified and listed, with the amount and price of each category. It's important that you itemize your inventory costs. Ask yourself what inventory do I need, what's the value, the rate of turnover, is there a seasonal build up and what's the lead time for reordering?

List any other needs such as the initial marketing & advertisement costs, signage or a business vehicle.

Your suppliers should be listed in such a way as to let the reader know what you are buying, from what supplier and the price. Also, make a statement as to why you selected this particular supplier by adding their credibility.

HOW I WILL ACHIEVE THE AMERICAN DREAM
WHO COULD HELP ME DETERMINE MY START-UP COSTS?

POINT 14: BUSINESS ASSETS

All owners who start up their business should have some assets to demonstrate a true commitment to their business. Many times there are some existing office contents, equipment or inventory that can be shown as collateral.

This is the time to identify and list all of the business assets that you may already have and are going to use in your operations. When you have completed the entire list of assets, then allocate a price value for each and add these together for your grand total of assets that should be included here in your Plan.

If you have other personal assets, then you may have to include some of these to guarantee your loan. However, do not pledge all of your personal assets because you may need some of these for expansion at a later time.

You can also research securing funds from angel investors or Venture Capitalists and their roles are quite similar. They are looking to invest in new start-up businesses that appear to have a great deal of growth potential. They lend you the money and to protect themselves, they take ownership of a percentage of your business. They usually want their money back quicker than a bank. and expect a higher level of profit.

Before going to meet with the loan officer seek the guidance of your financial advisor and bookkeeper about how to effectively negotiate a business loan.

HOW I WILL ACHIEVE THE AMERICAN DREAM
WHY SHOULD I SHOW SOME ASSETS IN MY PLAN?

POINT 15: FIXED MONTHLY EXPENSES

It's essential to list all of your anticipated fixed monthly expenses in your Plan. This is because you should determine how much you need to set aside each month to cover these expenses.

If your incoming revenue does not cover your anticipated fixed monthly expenses and leave a profit, then you need to reconsider your business operation's viability because showing a profit is your "bottom line". Your Plan should include all of your anticipated fixed monthly expenses such as the following:

Rent $

Utilities

Loan Repayment (if any)

Telephone & Cell Phones & Internet

Insurance

Dues & Subscriptions

Mailings

Waste or Trash Pick-up

Owner Draw or Salary

Salaries for Employees

Taxes

Total = $

HOW I WILL ACHIEVE THE AMERICAN DREAM
WHAT IF I DISCOVER THAT MY INCOMING MONTHLY REVENUES WILL NOT BE SUFFICIENT ENOUGH TO COVER MY ANTICIPATED MONTHLY EXPENSES AND WHO DO I CONTACT?

POINT 16: LOAN RATIONALE:

Recently, I polled several local loan officers about the kinds of loan requests that they are receiving. They all said that numerous potential entrepreneurs come in seeking a loan without a Business Action Plan. All of these loan officers said that they would not consider any loan request without a Business Plan.

I also had the same experiences because over 90% of all my new students lack a Plan and are not aware of how much money they really need to start-up. I explain that there will be no loans available until they complete their Plan.

Dr. Pat's Inside Secret:
If there is one single piece of advice I could give you in raising money, is that you determine how much capital you need, what will you do with every dollar, how long will you need this money for and how do you propose to pay it back.

Initially, if you decide that you don't need outside funding, you will still have to complete some segments of this point to successfully operate your business. There will be a future time when you will want to expand your business and then you will need to seek a loan.

A major mistake many entrepreneurs make is that they start the business beyond their means. They open, but lack one important asset and that is operating capital. When they haven't put aside sufficient working cash, then current bills can't be paid, their operation goes into a cash crisis and the business begins to wither. Without a "floating" supply of cash, a business will experience convulsions that distort, confuse, embarrass and alarm everyone concerned with this business.

I asked myself questions when preparing to seek my micro loan:

- What specific business am I in?
- What is my legal form of ownership?
- What are my experience & expertise in this field?
- Where is my location?
- Who and where are my customers?
- Why is my business superior to my competitors?
- What will I do with loan funds and how will I pay these back?

In addition, there were three essential questions that the loan officer expected me to respond to: what do I need financing for, what am I going to do with every dollar and how am I going to ensure that I can pay the loan back in an acceptable timeframe.

In considering which financial alternative is best for your business, it is important to draw on the experience and expertise your bookkeeper, banker and attorney who have already been through numerous start up ventures.

Dr. Pat's Inside Secret:
I stress here that you should never drain all of your liquid assets, but keep sufficient funds to maintain a healthy cash flow and allow for potential growth.

UNLOCK THE AMERICAN DREAM

One of the major concerns for many business owners today is how to access a loan when they have prior poor credit. The Small Business Administration (SBA) has various loan guarantee programs to provide financing for viable businesses that have potential, but can't qualify for traditional loans. When you go to the lending institutions, they may want SBA to grantee your loan in order to reduce the bank's risk.

Financing programs provided by SBA vary according to the borrower's need. Initially, the private lender determines whether a borrower's application is acceptable. If it is, the lender forwards the application and its credit analysis to the SBA. After the SBA review and approval, the lender makes the loan. The borrower then must pay the lender payments according to their loan agreement. You can find out more about various SBA loan programs by going on their web site at www.sba.gov.

If you are seeking a loan upfront then, explain that if the loan or investment is received it will enable your business to operate at a level needed to meet your conservative sales and profit margin goals and this loan can readily be paid back.

Your loan rationale must include the specific breakdown of what the funds will be used for such as: purchasing a building, renovations, furnishings, equipment, start-up inventory, initial advertisement, signage and operating capital.

No matter whether you are applying for a loan or not, the following data need to be completed and added to your Plan. The data should be prepared with your CPA and/or bookkeeper because the accuracy of these figures will reflect the success or failure of your business.

- *Working capital:* The minimum amount needed to operate your business for a six month period
- *Break Even Analysis:* The level of sales at which your total sales cover exactly your total costs and operating expenses; the point of zero profits
- *Three Year Pro Forma:* Your projections of the money coming in, money going out and your estimated financial status of your business for at least three years
- *Personal Income Statements for Three Years:*
  Do not hide any personal income information that is negative because the loan officer finds out anyways

Before your Plan goes anywhere, give a copy to two others to proof-read and make any comments. This document will say a great deal about you and your proposed business and this is the ultimate goal for creating your Master Plan.

POINT 17:BUSINESS ADVISORS

Business advisors are vital in providing continuing guidance and support for your growing company, so select them wisely.

Conversations with an entrepreneur winner: My mentor advised me to associate with people who think "winning" and know that the only one who could make me fail is myself!

You should select mentors who have the expertise and experience in your company's field to network and render advice. List the professionals that you will utilize to ensure that you have a strong and viable network of advisors to help ensure your success.

Famous Quote: Keep away from people who try to belittle your ambitions.
Small people always do that, but the really great ones make you feel that you too can become great
(Mark Twain, American Novelist, 1835-1910).

It's wise to add data about the advisors in your Plan:

Banker, Attorney, Insurance Agent & Other Mentors:

Name_____

Address _____

_____

Tele#_____

Email _____

COMPOSING YOUR BUSINESS ACTION PLAN:

Throughout the preceding text the points of your Plan have been elaborated on at length. The "ball is now in your court". It's time for you to create your Plan by completing the points in a structured manner showing how you will launch and establish your business. Until you do this, your Plan will simply be idle theory that remains in your head.

Writing your Plan serves two purposes: it forces you to write in a clear language about your operations and it becomes your document to present to those whose help you need to start-up.

Initially, the most difficult step is getting started on your Plan. Those who are really serious about starting a business quickly develop their Plan. Some who procrastinate seldom get their Plan "off the ground" and if they open without a Plan, most tend to fail.

HERE ARE SOME HINTS THAT I USED TO STRENGTHEN MY PLAN:

Point 1: Executive Summary:
An overview of the nature, ownership and location of my business

Point 2: Purpose & Legal Status:
Identified the legal status that my business and any other legal forms

Point 3: Management:
This point reflects strong management experience and expertise

Point 4: Personnel
The quality and commitment of my personnel was clearly detailed

Point 5: Product or Service Description
I explained my product/service and why customers will buy from me

Point 6: Customer Profile
This is where I stated that there are sufficient customers who can't live with out my product/service and I can realize a profit

Point 7: Location
I explained why my specific location is so important to my success

Point 8: Pricing
This is one of the most difficult areas. I explained exactly how I will make enough sales to generate a healthy profit

Point 9: Marketing & Advertisement
I provided details that I know how to find and reach my customers

Point 10: Competitors
Many entrepreneurs lack identifying their competitors and this makes loan officers uneasy, so I make certain that this is very clear

Point 11: Research & Development
I let the readers know that I will continue to research my line of business and its impact on the "bottom line"

Point 12: Targeting Your Market
Here in my Plan, I explain how I will target my specific market arena

Point 13: Initial Start-up Costs
I state what is specifically needed to start-up my business

Point 14: Business Assets
Some of my personal assets are cited here to show my commitment

Point 15: Anticipated Fixed Monthly Expenses
Remember the simple rule that more money comes in than goes out

Point 16: Business Advisors
I listed my business advisors and their qualities and expertise

Point 17: Loan Rationale
Loan officers want to know what you are going to do with every dollar and how you will pay the loan back

STAGE THREE

——— ✦ ———

BUSINESS SKILLS NEEDED TO REACH
FOR THE AMERICAN DREAM

THE STRONG BUSINESS skills cited here are those that are most vital to effectively starting and operating a successful business so that you can realize the American Dream.

I have taught these specific skills throughout the years while training hundreds of entrepreneur students and many have gone on to achieve the American Dream. You probably already have some of these skills, but you may want to incorporate some new ones so that you will be even more effectively skills-oriented.

Dr. Pat's Inside Secret:
I recommend that you learn all of the business skills that you can to add strength when operating your business and to effectively deal with your personnel and customers.

BUSINESS SKILLS #1: WINNING TRAITS

Let's commence this point by reviewing the winning business skills that I have complied through the years about highly successful entrepreneurs. These are my graduates that I have trained, mentored and coached as they strive to reach the American Dream:

Good Listener	**Sense of Humor**
Positive Thinker	**Creative Mind**
A Leader Who Loves Making Money	**Effective Communicator**
Prioritizes & Is A Change Agent	**Focused & A Risk Taker**
Problem Solver	**Expects Nothing But The Best**
Motivator	**Super Seller**
Analytical and Logical	**Achieves The Impossible**

Motivator & Team Player	Independent Thinker
Astute Decision Maker	Organized
Effectively Delegates	Time & Stress Manager

Trend Setter in the Business World

Successful entrepreneurs have control of their time and stress, are eager to try new ideas, take calculated risks and greet change as a challenge and not as a threat.

They overlap their work and play so much that they don't know if they are working or playing. They put their life on fast forward and eagerly look for "the next mountain to climb" to grow their business.

The common traits of less-than-successful entrepreneurs that I have seen throughout my twenty years of teaching entrepreneur programs are: most think that struggling is part of life and a noble profession. Stress is common and their life is full of drama, struggles and chaos.

Dr. Pat's Inside Secret:
Many entrepreneurs that I have seen tend to fail because they lack focus, are afraid of the added responsibilities and show excessive worry or fear. Stay alert and be aware of these signs.

Vince Lombardi, legendary football coach, once told his team that "Winning is 90% in your head". Those like my winners think that they will succeed and they do. They tend to be the cheerleader for their employees and realize that the harder it is to accomplish a goal, the sweeter it is when you achieve it.

The definition of a leader is "An action person who directs, commands, guides, conducts and performs" (Webster's Dictionary). Managing the business operations involves coordinating resources, performing managerial functions aimed at achieving coordination and establishing the purpose of the management process.

All of these functions involve:

- *Money*: **Awareness of available capital at all times**
- *Materials*: **Includes physical properties**
- *People*: **All those impacting the business**

The management process, as I defined it, involves finding a need to satisfy, identifying sufficient customers, researching the market arena and continuing to have a solid Business Action Plan to address your growth.

BUSINESS SKILLS #2: PERMITS, REGULATIONS, COPYRIGHTS AND TRADE MARKS

All business owners need to be aware of the regulations and permits that will impact their business operation. In addition, you may want to consider protecting your branding items through copyright or trademark.

It's critical that you seek the advice of an attorney about potential rules, regulations and requirements for your operations because going into business is such a litigious industry. You need to review the following:

Federal Identification Number (EIN):

One of the items that you will want is a Federal Employer Identification Number (EIN) when you assume operating your business. You will need the EIN to file you tax returns. When you become the new owner of an existing business, you can not use the former EIN, but must secure your own by contacting the IRS office.

PERMITS AND LICENSES:

The State Office of Business Permits and Regulatory Assistance provides information and assistance to owners operating within their state.

SALES TAX:

If your business sells goods or services, then you have to charge, collect and pay taxes. As a registered vendor doing business in most states, you will have to keep detailed records of all sales, rentals and transactions that are subject to sales taxes. Ask your financial advisor about the sales tax rules in your area. Remember that you are liable for the payment of these sales taxes whether you collect them or not.

SPECIAL TAXES:

Special taxes have been imposed in addition to the normal sales tax on things such as rental of cars, special hotel occupancy taxes and on lubricating oils in many states. Check these special taxes out with your financial advisor.

VENDOR REGISTRATION:

If your new business requires you to collect sales tax or if you buy or sell for resale purposes (wholesale distributor), then you must register as a vendor with the Tax Department at least twenty days before doing business. Rules, regulations and laws frequently change; so seek guidance from your financial person.

WITHHOLDING TAX & WAGE REPORTS:

One of your chief tax duties as an employer is to withhold income taxes from the wages of your employees and to report and pay the taxes withheld. You should confer with your financial advisor to be certain that you are correctly complying with these regulations.

WORKER'S COMPENSATION & DISABILITY BENEFITS:

As an employer, you have an obligation regarding the requirement of disability benefits and worker's compensation insurance. Information and forms are available through your insurance carrier.

COPYRIGHT:

Copyright is a form of protection for your printed materials provided by the Laws of the United States (Title 17, U.S. Code) to the authors of "original works of authorship". This protection is available to both published and unpublished works. For further information, consult the copyright law or your attorney.

PATENT:

One legal protection option is filing for a patent that will protect your original device or prototype. You need to seek a patent attorney in this case.

TRADE MARK OR SERVICE MARK:

These are used to guard your product's name, logo, symbol or figure. Initially, you should invest the time to review trade mark and service mark basics to avoid mistakes that may cost you time, money and potentially your legal rights later on.

WHAT I LEARNED
HOW CAN I LEARN ABOUT WHAT RULES AND REGULATIONS I SHOULD FOLLOW?

SHOULD I RESEARCH COPYRIGHT AND/OR TRADE MARK DATA THAT MAY APPLY TO MY BUSINESS?

BUSINESS SKILLS #3: WHAT TO ASK BEFORE SIGNING A LEASE

Many new business owners want to lease their site and its imperative that your attorney be directly involved with this lease from the onset. Do not sign a lease unless your attorney reviews and approves this document. Below are some of the questions that you need to ask before the lease is signed:

- How much is the monthly rent and is it negotiable? If you have to clean, paint or add some essentials that require the outlay of your money negotiate being compensated.
- How long is the lease for? Can you can afford to continue paying it if you go out of business or move to a larger site.
- Can I sublease any of my space? Most landlords will not let you do this so it's better that you know this upfront.
- How much will my rent go up each year? You should assess whether or not you can afford it over time.
- What services am I provided with such as lawn care, snow plowing etc. Don't let this come as a surprise cost to you.
- What happens if your landlord goes broke? Your attorney should add a standard recognition of non-disturbance.
- Who's responsible for insurance?
- If improvements or repairs are needed then who pays?
- Who else can move into your immediate area? What happens if a new business comes in and takes all of the parking spaces, creates a high level of noise or has unsavory customers?
- Can you renew the lease and an option to buy the building?

WHAT I LEARNED

WHY IS IT IMPORTANT THAT MY ATTORNEY REVIEW AND AGREE WITH THE TERMS IN MY LEASE BEFORE I SIGN IT?

BUSINESS SKILLS #4: SETTING YOUR GOALS

Dr. Pat's Inside Secret:

Goals are merely wishes put to writing that need specific objectives that can be readily measured to determine if you have met your goals.

I highly recommend that you establish your business goals well before you even you start your business. You also need specific objectives to go along with each goal so that you can measure your success in achieving these.

Famous Quote: Don't ask what the world needs. Ask what makes you come alive and go do it!
What the world needs are people who have come alive like you
(Howard Thurman, American Author, 1899-1981).

The owner of McDonalds, Ray Kroc, knew exactly what his business goals and objectives were before he even started this venture. In his mind, he envisioned every activity that could impact the success and growth of his operation.

To secure a stable future for all those connected with your company, long term goals that represent your future growth and expansions should be established. For example; a goal might be to have a healthy, successful company that will become the leader in customer service and has a loyal customer following.

Bear in mind to research and know what your most important company strengths and core competencies are going to be. Think about the research that has been and will be conducted to grow your company in your industry arena.

I achieved the following to validate that I'm successful:

- Won Trade Industry Awards
- Secured the major market share in this region
- Became involved in community projects

WHAT I LEARNED

WHY SHOULD I DEVELOP SPECIFIC GOALS AND OBJECTIVES?

A common question that I ask when talking with someone who is starting their own business is: "Are family members going to be involved in your business"? If the response is yes, then the work begins for me! The designated manager of the family must start off on the right foot by being prepared to handle the family members who are going to be directly involved in the operations.

Management problems occur in every business, but when it comes to "our" business instead of "my" business, then the problems are far different. When family members come together to operate a business, emotions frequently interfere with the decision-making process.

Conflict and problems sometimes overflow into all facets of the operations when relatives observe the business from different viewpoints. Like any other business, employees must have the qualifications to do their job, have job descriptions and periodic evaluations. These are only a few of the challenges that need to be address to avoid family problems from emerging.

If relatives are stockholders or silent partners, they tend to put profit making activities far above capital improvements, purchase of needed equipment or investing in more inventory. Sometimes relatives will frown upon hiring new employees, even though it is vital to the growth of the company. Some relatives are reluctant to put profits back into the business. Problems are further compounded if the relative has no talent for money or business.

When relatives are directly involved in the daily business operations, they tend to consider major issues in light of growth, production sales and employees. For the person who has to manage the family business, the most important factor is to recognize the relatives' emotions and make every attempt to keep them under control.

Many times it's difficult to assess relatives' skills and abilities when another relative is calling them lazy and undependable. Emotions not only affect the family working together, but other employees too. Uncontrolled family conflict tends to spread like "wild fire". If you are the one delegated to be the manager, then you had better be assertive and tough enough to handle bickering and personal conflicts, because these are inevitable.

Famous Quote: It is amazing what you can accomplish if you do not care who gets the credit (Harry Truman, US President, 1884-1972).

Many entrepreneurs throughout the years are those who are going to be the "head' of a family business, so I created the following tips:

1. Manage by assuming that all of the family members will be working toward profits and growth?

2. Develop your Organizational Chart:
You need just a simple chart that shows the chain of command. This may be enough to clarify who's in charge.

3. Adhere to Jobs Descriptions:
Family members should all have a clear understanding what their jobs entails. This will prevent conflict and help in resolving misunderstandings.

4. Never Do Anything That Someone Else Can Do For You:
If you are designated as the key person, then refrain from doing routine tasks that can be done by your employees. You are there to manage and effectively operate this business with an eye on attaining the American Dream.

5. Take Action to Reduce Costs:
Family members should come together regularly to brainstorm about reducing costs. Costs must be kept in line to continue a profitable operation. Quality, service, excellence and attention to customers should always come first.

6. Outline Policies and Procedures:
The best products and/or services in the world can run into difficulty with distribution if policies and procedures are not right for them. One strategy is to check on your competitors to see if they are operating more effectively.

7. Planning for Succession in the Event of Your Untimely Demise:
As the designated leader of the family business, it is up to you to make certain that a smooth transition occurs if something happens to you.

Every manager has to work hard at initiating and maintaining sound management principles, but this is even more difficult when family members are involved in the operation. Operating a family business is a real challenge, but in the end it will leave your family legacy that shows you have achieved the American Dream.

WHAT I LEARNED
WHAT SPECIFIC LEADERSHIP SKILLS WILL I NEED TO BE AN EFFECTIVE LEADER IF I'M SELECTED AS THE HEAD OF OUR FAMILY BUSINESS?

BUSINESS SKILLS #6: BUYING AN EXISTING BUSINESS

Buyers of a business usually have one of three motives: (1) Access to new technologies or new markets, (2) Financial gain or (3) To buy the business and operate it. Buying an existing business can be a simple shortcut to establishing your own business, but it has its pros and cons that need to be discussed beforehand with your team of the attorney, banker and accountant.

To determine the selling price of a business, a valuation assessment report must be prepared by the seller and reviewed by the buyer and the team. This report eliminates the guesswork and the painful trial and error method of determining the price.

Businesses are frequently purchased in total that includes equipment, fixtures, inventory and office set-up/supplies. As the buyer, you can easily go off course by selecting a business that is already ill fated, perhaps in a less than desirable location and/or has gained a poor reputation.

ADVANTAGES OF BUYING AN EXISTING BUSINESS:

If the following are positive then you may want to purchase:

- Acquiring a well established business operation
- An above-average customer base
- First-class employees
- Premium inventory on hand
- High quality equipment with long term warranties
- A first-rate reputation and "track record"

DISADVANTAGES OF BUYING A BUSINESS:

Some disadvantages of buying an existing business are:

- Old and obsolete inventory,
- A business that is over-priced
- Caters to the wrong type of customers
- The owner takes customers with them
- Deteriorating site
- Poor employees
- Current owner has a bad reputation or poor credit

STEPS TO TAKE:

1. Get Your Banker, Accountant and Attorney involved upfront:

Assessing the three-year financials of the current operation that you want to buy, inspecting the federal tax records and reviewing the state sales tax records are essential to review with your advisors.

2. What is the "good will" of the seller?

Talk with the seller's customers, bankers, neighboring business operators and suppliers. If the seller isn't willing to give you the names of these contacts, then walk away from this deal.

3. Ask the question; "Why do they want to sell"?

Does this business venture appear to fit in with all the data that you received? Does it seem genuine and make sense to you? Ask more questions and don't be shy because it's your hard earned money.

4. What are you really getting for your money?

Has the local Codes Department been contacted and is there a variance in place so that once the purchase is final, you can operate the same kind of business. Just because the current business is operating as a café doesn't mean that you can purchase it and assume that you can operate a café too.

The signage comes with the deal, but are you going to change the name and add another unexpected cost. Are the furnishings what you really want or could you do better by purchasing new ones.

5. What's left after the purchase?

Consider what you are getting for your money and would you be farther ahead starting this business from scratch? One area that you should be concerned about is whether or not there are warranties covering the major appliances. Also, you must look at your cash flow once the final payment is made and whether or not you have ample cash to operate the business.

WHAT I LEARNED
WHAT SHOULD I LOOK FOR IF I WANTED TO PURCHASE AN EXISTING BUSINESS?

WHO WOULD I INVOLVE IN THIS DECISION-MAKING PROCESS?

BUSINESS SKILLS #7: TYPES OF PERSONALITIES

Soon after opening my first business, I realize that people with different personalities can and do directly impact the success or failure of any business. These people are managers, employees, suppliers or customers. I decided that if I was aware of what makes people "tick" and applied this knowledge to my business then there maybe a better chance of my succeeding in business.

All people (including ourselves) commonly demonstrate certain characteristics that place them in one of the four categories listed below. True, there is some overlap, but usually a person will exhibit more characteristics in one or two categories. The point that I'm making here is; what kind of personalities could strengthen my operations and lead to my business success.

Dr. Pat's Inner Secret:
When I decided to hire my first employees, I researched and soon discovered that there are numerous types of personalities that comprise society (M. Brounstein, 2013). Realizing that people, with their various personality traits, would impact my business, I decided to hire by using the four major personality types which are: Critical Thinkers, People Pleasers, Go-Getters and Entrepreneur Visionaries.

Critical Thinkers exhibit rigid ways, are "all business", quiet observers, everything must be in place, are well organized, serious, analytical, overly neat, conservative dressers, structured in their actions and think before speaking. These are the personnel that you want to help you handle your money and maintain your financial records.

People Pleasers are humanistic, friendly, outgoing, like warm colors, good natured, idealistic, committed to their values, loyal, dislike conflicts, accepting in nature and tolerant. They are very people-oriented and will keep your customers coming back time and time again. You have to be alert that they don't waste too much just talking.

Go Getters are organizers, overachievers, their life is as upscale as they can get, tend to get jobs done quickly (although not always right). They are insensitive in nature; stay focused and have little time for "small talk". These people will help you stay on target and make you money, but are usually not very customer-oriented.

Entrepreneur Visionaries are usually outgoing, set unrealistic goals most of the time, disregard deadlines, are innovators and think "out of the box". They are original in every way and others view them as rather unusual.

These people are great to have on your team because they bring about new and innovative ideas that tend to result in profit-bearing changes that keep your business a "head above" your competitors. Visionaries are the most positive employees on your team. However, you needed to harness their ideas and keep them on a winning track.

Who Am I?

You may want to look at your own personality traits so that you can determine what you are capable of while handling the growth of your business.

Famous Quote: The power of imagination is infinite
(John Muir, Environmentalist, 1838-1914).

I know that I may never become a full-blown critical thinker, but I do have some basic skills to make my financial manager think that I know something about my finances. I'm a people pleaser and a go getter at heart. I'm still trying to become even more of an entrepreneur visionary to add strength and resiliency to my American Dream image.

Famous Quote: It's never too late to be what you might have been
(George Eliot, Author, 1819-1880).

WHAT I LEARNED
WHAT IS MY SPECIFIC TYPE OF PERSONALITY?

HOW WILL MY PERSONALITY TRAITS HELP OR HINDER MY SUCCESS?

My definition of a problem is anything that gets in the way of succeeding in my business operations.

Dr. Pat's Inside Secret:
Early on in business, I developed and applied the Issue Paper to handle problems. This is still a very effective tool for addressing problems and I continue to use it today.
The Issue Paper is comprised of writing a clear statement of pertinent and factual information about a specific problem that needs to be solved. It helps me take positive action very quickly to address a specific problem that emerges in my operations.

Here are the eight questions that comprise my Issue Paper:

1. What is the problem? (magnitude, critical issues, causes)
2. Will this problem happen again or is it a one-time problem?
3. What is the desired state that I wish to achieve and how will this be measured?
4. What are the interacting factors or concurrent activities?
5. Who else has an interest in this problem?
6. What are the constraints or limitations?
7. What are the alternatives and can I prioritize these?
8. What immediate action should I take and what is the recommended follow-up?

The value of the Issue Paper is that it focuses on the "real" problem rather than symptoms, creates systematic analysis of the problem, stimulates the generation of alternatives, exposes information gaps and creates a frank discussion about a specific problem and identifies potential alternatives for handling this problem.

Famous Quote: In order to be effective, truth must penetrate like an arrow and that is likely to hurt (Wei Wu Wei, British Philosopher, 1895-1986).

If your business day is frequently filled with crises and "fire fighting", then you must become proactive in these situations. Crisis management is reacting to problems as they occur. Start by taking proactive steps to avoid or limit the consequences associated with a potential problem.

Remember Murphy's Law that states: "If anything can go wrong it will, nothing is as simple as it seems and everything takes longer than we think".

You can handle most situations by sound pre-planning, continuous monitoring of your operations and not over reacting until you assess the real problems that occur.

WHAT I LEARNED
WHAT STRATEGIES WILL I USE TO SOLVE EMERGING PROBLEMS?

BUSINESS SKILLS #9: TIME MANAGEMENT

"Planning in advance what is to be done in the future" is the core of effective time management and requires three steps:

- Prioritize what you (1) **_have_** to get done, (2) **_want_** to get done and (3) would **_like to_** get done someday (no rush),
- Who could I delegate to (should I delegate or not) and
- How will I know when the job is done?

Everybody says that they don't have enough time, yet every day is the same 24 hours for everyone. It isn't a matter of not having enough time; it's how we manage it. It's critical to set priorities and use time to our best advantage, if we want to succeed in business. We need to stay focused on what really has to get done.

There is a simple theory that we all have times (hours) when we are more productive than other times. Think about when you like to work and when you are more productive. Some of us are "morning people" who like to get up real early and work. Others are evening people who could work all night. When you have to do something important, consider your best time to do it. The point here is to implement the best way to use your time productively.

Handling Mail: One problem facing a sole owner is the vast amount of incoming mail. I recommend that you handle this mail once by replying immediately, delegating or discarding it.

Telephone Calls: When you're going it alone, respond to a phone call by asking yourself: Why is this person calling, how much time can I devote to talking and then stick to this timeframe. Use an assertive closure technique, such as "I know how busy you are, so I'll let you go" and that will usually works.

Drop In Visitors: When someone walks in and you have a lot to do, greet them, connect and then walk them to the door. Some entrepreneurs eliminate all of their chairs to discourage visitors.

Emails: Set up a structured schedule to frequently review your emails. Read them and respond immediately to as many as you can.

Dr. Pat's Inside Secret:
I discovered that if I do my daily work plan before I leave each night, my work the next day is accomplished in a much more structured manner without the usual headaches that come from "hit or miss" random planning.

DAILY WORK PLAN

Your daily work plan is your structured "To Do" List.

Date	Rank Importance	Time Needed	Completed
1.			
2.			
3.			
4.			
5.			
6.			
7.			
8.			
9.			
10.			
11.			

WHAT I LEARNED

HOW CAN I BE CERTAIN THAT I'M NOT WASTING MY TIME BECAUSE TIME IS MONEY?

HOW WILL I MANAGE MY TIME TO BE PRODUCTIVE?

BUSINESS SKILLS #10: STRESS MANAGEMENT

My Master's thesis and Doctoral dissertation were both on: "The Development Of An Exemplary Model For A Stress Training Program for Managers/Supervisors In Business, Industry, Education and Health Care Organizations".

Stress is nothing new to humanity and it is commonly referred to as human suffering. The definition of stress in my doctoral dissertation is simply; "problems on the outside causing you problems inside". Stress is the result of how we perceive a person, place or event.

The causes of stress are called stressors, which are people, places or situations. Stressors can be handled in one of three ways:

(1) Flee or walk away,

(2) Fight or confront or

(3) Float and take time to analyze the situation.

Research shows that the major stressors are people. Many of these people could be your customers with a complaint or even your employees. The most effective way to handle a complaint is to hear the person out, ask what they think should be done and then come to a mutual agreement.

**Famous Quote: Remember that everyone you meet is afraid of something,
loves something and has lost something
(H. Jackson Brown Jr., American Author, 1940 to present).**

DR. PAT'S QUESTIONNAIRE

Rate yourself how you typically react in the situations listed below.

1- Never 2-Seldom 3-Sometimes 4-Frequent 5-Always

	1	2	3	4	5
1. Do you try to do as much as possible in the least amount of time?	1	2	3	4	5
2. Are you impatient with delays?	1	2	3	4	5
3. Do you have to win at games to enjoy yourself?	1	2	3	4	5
4. Are you upset when interrupted?	1	2	3	4	5
5. Do you constantly strive to better your position or achievements?	1	2	3	4	5
6. Do you constantly need praise from others?	1	2	3	4	5
7. Are you overly critical of the way others work?	1	2	3	4	5
8. Do you have the habit of looking at your watch?	1	2	3	4	5
9. Do you spread yourself too thin in terms of time?	1	2	3	4	5
10. Do you have the habit of doing more than one thing at a time?	1	2	3	4	5
11. Do you ever get angry or irritable?	1	2	3	4	5
12. Do you have a tendency to talk quickly or hasten the conversation?	1	2	3	4	5
13. Do you consider yourself hard-driving?	1	2	3	4	5
14. Do others consider you hard-driving?	1	2	3	4	5
15. Do you have a tendency to get involved in multiple projects?	1	2	3	4	5
16. Do you have a lot of deadlines in your work?	1	2	3	4	5
17. Do you feel vaguely guilty if you relax or get out of the office at lunch?	1	2	3	4	5
18. Do you take on too many responsibilities?	1	2	3	4	5

STRESS METER

Very Little Stress = 18-27   **Low Borderline Stress = 28-45**

High Borderline Stress = 46-62   **Highly Stress Prone = 63-90**

STRATEGIES FOR COPING WITH STRESS:

- Address one problem at a time and take some action
- Forget perfection; just get the job done right the first time!
- Worry less because the things that you worry about most will probably never happen
- Bury yesterday. Learn by these stressful experiences, be done with them and consider it over
- Develop new friendships by networking
- Learn to say "no", stop being super-human
- Manage your time because no one is going to do it for you
- Relax sometimes and work smarter not harder
- Roll with the punches by counting to ten
- Accept change as an opportunity and not a threat
- Think positive when the "going gets tough"
- Take specific steps to control your business and your life

WHAT I LEARNED
HOW CAN I IDENTIFY MY MAJOR STRESSORS?

HOW CAN I LEARN HOW TO HANDLE THE SPECIFIC STRESSORS THAT COME WITH OPERATING MY BUSINESS?

BUSINESS SKILLS #11: BURNOUT

Burnout is a destructive syndrome that creeps up on entrepreneur over a long period of time. It impacts those who care too much about their commitments. It's when life loses its meaning and damage strikes both the physical and emotional well-being. It's the high cost of "over caring", usually, attempting to reach unrealistic goals in your business and in your life as a whole.

Along with operating your business comes the chance of burnout caused by long hours, overwhelming business obstacles and just the stress of competing over the years.

Burnout is a destructive syndrome that slowly creeps up on people. With burnout comes negative attitude, a feeling of continuing exhaustion, life loses its meaning, job helplessness and high irritability that doesn't go away.

**Famous Quote: I have learned to be content in whatever circumstances I am in
(Phillipians 4:11).**

You should begin to avoid burnout as soon as you launch your venture to ensure a long and happy life until you sell. I set realistic goals and continued to think "out of the box" so that I could avoid burnout. Ensuring that my business and personal life had equal time was a great stress reliever.

I learn from my mistakes and bury these as "learning experiences". I play by the rule that stress is my body's reaction to a demand made upon it and if left unresolved, then burnout will creep in.

"No person is an island" was coined many years ago and still holds true today. We all need a support team to help with our stress so that we can avoid burnout.

WHAT I LEARNED
WHAT STEPS CAN I TAKE TO AVOID BURNOUT FROM THE VERY START OF OPERATING MY BUSINESS?

BUSINESS SKILLS #12: SUPER SELLING

How you look and carry yourself is vital to your success. Initially, I start with the "top to bottom" profile of the successful entrepreneur. This is an assessment tool that I created several years ago when I, myself, wanted to attract customers (and money) for a new business venture that I was launching. You start at the top with your hair and proceed down to your shoes to determine if you have created a super selling image that reflects your business.

It is up to you to track the latest professional image so that you are up-to-date at all times. I always dress for success because the leader of a major company may walk in at anytime.

**Famous Quote: How does one become a butterfly? You must want to fly so much
that you are willing to give up being a caterpillar
(Trina Paulus, Author, 1931 to present).**

Routinely, we all carry a briefcase and this is one of the categories that have a rating of high importance, yet is given little attention. One of the most extravagant purchases that I have ever made was buying the red Hermes designer briefcase. People always cast admiring glances at it and this seems to lend additional credibility to my image.

Once you have achieved a winning appearance, put the time and efforts into keeping it in order to climb the ladder of success. When I get ready to leave the house everyday I look into the mirror and say; "Would I buy from me and do I look the part of a highly successful entrepreneur"?

**Famous Quote: Failure is the condiment that gives success its flavor
(Truman Capote, Dramatist, 1924-1984).**

If you want to sell your products or services, then you have to get rid of the fears and gain confidence by believing in yourself. Associate with "winners" and become the expert who knows all about their business and customers. To gain stronger speaking power, lower your voice an octave, avoid being the mumbler or rambler and pilot-test your conversation with family and friends until you get it "right".

WHAT I LEARNED
HOW CAN I IMPROVE MY OUTER IMAGE TO RADIATE SUCCESS?

HOW CAN I CHANGE MY INNER IMAGE TO REFLECT CONFIDENCE?

BUSINESS SKILLS #13: EFFECTIVE COMMUNICATIONS

Who benefits from effective communications and the answer is everyone! The way you should communicate depends on the current situation and the outcome that you want to achieve.

Dr. Pat's Inside Secret:
Communication is effective only if it gets the results you intended.

THE ELEVATOR SPEECH:

All of my entrepreneurs learn and practice their Elevator Speech from day one. Suppose that you are in an elevator and someone asks about your business. What do you tell people about your business in a couple of minutes when they ask?

To respond to this, you are to write a 30 second commercial about your business, its product or service in about 85 words. Memorize and practice it so that you are prepared to recite it when any and all opportunities arise.

THE FATAL MISTAKE:

Through the years there is one fatal behavior that I see over and over again in some of my entrepreneur less-successful students. Many of them fail to listen to the advice of experts in the field of business. Stakes are too high not to listen to these experts. The reality check in achieving the American Dream is to listen, listen, listen!

**Famous Quote: Don't persuade, defend or interrupt.
Be curious, be conversational, be real and above all, listen
(Elizabeth Lesser, American Writer, age unknown).**

My role as an entrepreneur instructor is to assist students with identifying their goals, translating these into business strategies and outlining the steps necessary to successfully achieve the American Dream.

There is a lot at risk if entrepreneurs don't listen because they run the chance of failing at the "hardest game in town", which is succeeding in their business.

I recommend that anyone thinking of going into business listen and follow through on the advice of the experts. Don't be offended when you're told that your business goals are unrealistic and that you need to go back to the drawing board. Students who don't listen will settle for less, work longer, harder and experience crippling stress.

**Famous Quote: Say what you want to say when you have the chance.
My greatest regrets are the things I did not do, the opportunities missed and the things unsaid
(Jim Keller, Blues Artist, and no age given).**

We all need effective communication techniques when handling individual face-to-face communications, with telephone calls, when writing to someone and at group meetings.

Face-to-face is the major two-way conversation that happens almost everyday while you're in business. You may speak to an employee or a customer and there are certain skills that you need to successfully achieve your desired outcome.

**Dr. Pat's Inside Secret:
The most effective technique that I use is face-to-face communications so that I can see the reaction of the listener and adjust my comments to get what I want.**

Some of my general rules to achieve effective face-to-face communications are to listen and talk in turns, ask questions for clarification and repeat what you want to communicate.

**Famous Quote: We read the world wrong and say that it deceives us
(R. Tagore, Novelist, 1861-1941).**

Always watch for the following tell-tale signs while listening, but don't take these for gospel:
- Open hands and unbutton coat = an open person
- Sitting straight and steeple their hands = confidence
- Crossing their arms = suspicion
- Clearing their throat or rubbing nose or eyes = suspicion
- Pointing a finger or speaking short = frustration

WHAT I LEARNED

HOW CAN I PREPARE MY ELEVATOR SPEECH?

WHAT COULD I CHANGE TO COMMUNICATE MORE EFFECTIVELY?

BUSINESS SKILLS #14: PRODUCTIVE MEETINGS

The most frequent meetings are small assemblies that are taking place every day in companies around the world. Most of the time these gatherings are a waste of time. If this is the case, then why do we have so many of these? Some of these assemblies are ego trips or means of spreading responsibility. Organized in-house meetings that I conduct can be the most effective way to handle problems, motivate people, communicate information or assign some new tasks or clarify existing tasks.

Dr. Pat's Inside Secret:

Many years ago, I created an effective way to produce outstanding outcomes when conducting a meeting. I developed the "Z" method and used it with my employees to handle any problems that arose. It worked out very well at bringing effective closure to my problems. I labeled it: "Who's got the "Z" and I still use it today.

This is a simple method that I use to get the most out of a meeting. I start by assigning the "Z" to one of my staff for an upcoming meeting. This person sets up the meeting with me and assumes the role of sending out the agenda that denotes the subject matter to be discussed. During the meeting I'm just there to listen. After the meeting the "Z" generates a report to me of the outcomes.

This may appear that I have lost control of my operation, but this is not so. The "Z" method is a great way to get everyone who works for me involved in my operations. It even helps to solve some of my emerging problems. It's an opportunity to observe my employees in action at solving problems. It's amazing what you get when you seek staff input!

Famous Quote: What may be done at any time will be done at no time (Scottish Proverb).

WHAT I LEARNED

WHAT ARE THE BENEFITS OF USING THE "Z" METHOD?

Years ago, I defined the term "Customerization" as the ability to react positively to a series of assumptions about my customers and everything that impacts their satisfaction.

I always ask myself if I have as many customers as I want, are they loyal, do my employees know what our customers want and can we react rapidly to their demands or needs. One role that I play often is observing how my employees handle our customers.

IRATE CUSTOMERS:

Another one of my roles is teaching aspiring entrepreneurs how to effectively handle irate customers. This is so important to the success of any business. The scenario includes: an employee who listens to the irate customer and everyone needs to stay calm. Then there is the fact-finding period when it's decided if an apology by the employee is due or not. The employee applies the rule of: "here's what I'm going to do" in hopes of reaching an amicable agreement so that this customer will be happy and will continue to come back.

Let's face it, things do happen and we can't always prevent a problem from occurring so we had better be proactive enough to save the day and the customer.

Dr. Pat's Inside Secret:
Customers are made of gold and if you have them, you have a gold mine.

I developed a plan many years ago to train my managers, employees and anyone else that impact my operations. It was the following advice for everyone involved in my business:

1. Everyone must be "customer oriented" and be aware of our customers' wants and needs at all times.
2. We must keep the profits growing by putting customers' wants and needs first because they generate the profits.
3. You can't read a customer's mind so then listen carefully to what they are saying. Constantly be tuned into your customer's signals so that you don't miss out on what could drive greater success.
4. You have to be able to react rapidly by considering new products/services or profits could be lost.
5. Business is built on customers and without them you will have no profits. It's as simple as that! The most important element is customer satisfaction.

According to the American Society of Quality Control, customers:

Move or die	4%
Influenced by their friends	5%
Lured away by competition	9%
Dissatisfied with products or services	14%
Turned off by attitude or indifference by management or employees	68%*

All employees should remember that the first impression is the only impression and this is aimed at pleasing and keeping customers.

Dr. Pat's Inside Secret:
Satisfied customers today guarantee your paycheck tomorrow.

WHAT I LEARNED
HOW CAN I KEEP MY CUSTOMERS COMING BACK AND WHY?

BUSINESS SKILLS #16: BALANCING HOME LIFE & BUSINESS

Balancing your home, family and work isn't easy. It can be a challenge that can be handled by your ability to effectively prioritize not only your business needs, but also what's important in your personal life.

Dr. Pat's Inside Secret:
I say to entrepreneurs that if you organize your day, the rest is "child's play" and you will
free up time for your family.

Your family will usually accept your work schedule as long as you keep them in the loop of knowing what is going on in your busy schedule. Ask your family for help and it's amazing what they will do for you.

Blend your business and personal responsibilities to get the most out of life. There is never enough time in anyone's life, so consider the direct path to achieving what you desire by astute planning.

Famous Quote: The price of anything is the amount of life you exchange for it
(Henry David Thoreau, American Philosopher, 1817-1862).

DR. PAT'S CLOSING REMARKS TO STAGE THREE:

We are at the closure of this stage and many valuable business skills have been identified that will help you reach for the American Dream.

Famous Quote: Here is the test to find out whether your mission on Earth is finished:
if you're alive, it isn't
(Richard Bach, American Author, 1936 to present).

Let's recapture the traits of an entrepreneur winner that you can use on your path to operating a successful business:

Good Listener	Astute Decision Maker
A Leader Who Loves Making Money	Effective Communicator
Prioritizes & Is A Change Agent	Focused & Organized
Problem Solver	Expects Nothing But The Best
Motivator	Super Seller
Analytical and Logical	Achieves The Impossible
Motivator & Team Player	Independent Thinker

Famous Quote: If we listened to our intellect, we'd never have a love affair. We'd never have a friendship. We'd never go into business, because we'd be too cynical. Well, that's nonsense. You've got to jump off cliffs all the time and build your wings on the way down (Annie Dillard, American Author, 1945 to present).

Now that you have gotten this far, it's time to put all that you learned into creating your very own Plan and launching your business because success comes with overcoming challenges, staying focused and plenty of hard work.

GOOD LUCK MY FRIEND, BECAUSE LUCK ALSO ENTERS INTO THE WINNING EQUATION!

———— ❧ ————

BUSINESS ACTION PLAN

BEST BBQ
Morey Best, B.A, MS
Culinary & BBQ Specialist

123 Any St.
City, State Zip
Tele: (123) 456-7890

EXECUTIVE SUMMARY

BEST BBQ will be established by Morey Best, as the sole owner and proprietor. Currently, this business venture is being incorporated by the attorney, Robert Lawrence.

The purpose of this company is to offer home-made BBQ food items created from secret family recipes. Initially, this business will be mobile because we will take our products to various sites to serve our customers in the good weather. This mobile unit has already been constructed by the XXX Company that specializes in mobile food units.

There will be a wide variety of smoke-able meats from delicious and tender brisket to our flavorful BBQ pulled pork. Every meat is prepared using the family secret homemade rubs and sauces that brings a variety of new and exciting flavors.

In the warm months, customers will be served onsite at various locations such as: State Fairs, shopping centers and other places where groups of people gather and want to eat outstanding BBQ items and other home-made foods. There appears to be no other mobile business venture of this sort in the immediate surroundings that caters specifically to the BBQ crowd. When fall comes, this operation will operate downtown in a site that the family owns and they will lease it to Morey.

Imagine enjoying some of the most delicious BBQ style foods, drinks and pastries by coming to our mobile food concession unit. Morey has the culinary expertise and experience to launch this business.
BEST BBQ was created in response to these markets:

- Start-up opportunities exist for this exciting BBQ food business
- There is a need for the efficient distribution of unique and high quality food in efficient methods to serve this overlooked market
- We have numerous potential customers who will be willing to patronize our food concession and continue to return
- Additional prospective customers who are frequently looking for our type of foods have been contacted and are interested in coming to our onsite food concession in the summer and the downtown site in the winter months.

Over the past ten months, Morey has researched this idea, found a need and is creating a Business Action Plan (Plan) to ensure a profit germinating company. The first step was to purchase the mobile unit with some of Morey's savings.

Currently, the focus of BEST BBQ is to effectively achieve profitability by offering a unique and new approach of selling BEST BBQ foods via our mobile unit. The concept is in the early stage of extensive research and planning and to this point the following has been accomplished:

- Several summer food concession sites have now been reserved
- Our full-service mobile food truck has been delivered
- The winter location has been identified and leased
- Competitors are now being identified and researched
- Marketing & Advertisement strategies are being created

MANAGEMENT

Owner & Chief Operating Officer (CEO):

Morey Best, sole owner of this company, has over ten years of experience in various BBQ culinary and management roles. These essential skills will be responsible for the successful operations of this business. Recipes for BEST BBQ foods have been past down through several generations.

Job descriptions have been developed for three employees besides the owner. Morey will assume management duties, employee relations and any other managerial duties, as these emerge. Once this business venture is underway, Morey will manage this operation on a full-time basis, with the assistance of two family members and three employees.

Chief Financial Officer (CFO):

Morey has contacted a local book keeper, who will assume the role of financial advisor for this company. This professional will oversee the financial bookkeeping from the very start-up, as this is necessary from the very onset of this business in order to be aware of the profitability margin. On a regular basis, this financial advisor will oversee the financial operations, accounts payable and receivable and the interaction with any auditors.

Marketing Consultant:

Morey is in the process of researching and will contract with a marketing consultant that has the specific experience and expertise to effectively market his mobile business operations.

PERSONNEL

Once we are underway this spring, three well-trained employees will be hired to kick off this business. Morey believes very strongly in technical, financial, business and the pursuit of excellence. He will develop job descriptions for all employees, monitor and periodically evaluate them.

These new employees have already been identified because they have the culinary experience and expertise to become part of our culinary team. They will be trained by Morey who has the experience in this type of culinary BBQ operations.

PRODUCT DESCRIPTION

BEST BBQ will offer fresh and sought-after food dishes that are the best of authentic BBQ style, along with other food and drink items:

Special BEST BBQ ribs, chicken, pork and other meat specialties

Homemade Baked Beans		**French Fries**
Pulled Pork	**Corm Bread**	**Variety Homemade Chips**
BBQ Steak Sandwiches	**Cole Slaw**	**Variety of BBQ Subs**
A full range of Healthy Drinks		**Southern Short Cake Desserts**

<u>BEST BBQ Sandwiches will include:</u>

**Peppers, Onions, Cheese
Home-made BEST BBQ Sauces
Special seasonings**

LOCATION

This business will operate at various locations during the summer months in the XXX regions. These locations will be at busy sites and Fairs where hundreds of potential customers come all day and evening.

There will be numerous buyers because we are at a point of immediate and quality service of our BEST BBQ lines. The selected locations will be desirable because these will have a high rate of traffic and each location will have the necessary setting to effectively operate this venture. Sites will have easy access, be safe and have ample parking.

Planning is now underway to open in the cold months in a downtown site that the family currently owns. The renovations are being completed by family members who will then lease it to Morey. It is anticipated that we will open downtown the first week in November and continue year around from then on.

PRICING

Before we set the price for our BEST BBQ foods and other items, we will research all the similar prices that are current with our competitors. Pricing will be determined on a unit basis for all food and drink items. The charge per item will be computed by taking into consideration the cost per raw food item, each specific drink and dessert unit and the level of profit we want to achieve that will also depend on what the market will bear.

Pricing will be determined after we cost out each of our items to be sold. We will also research what the market price is for a comparable food item by our competitors. At this price, it will be concluded that for all but the lowest sales projections, each food line should and will turn a healthy profit. As a unique home-made mobile food company, we will be able to keep our margins high, allowing us to provide internal financing for future growth possibilities.

HEALTHY ENVIRONMENTAL PLAN

We will be closely monitoring all products that we use or dispose of to determine if any hazardous materials could possibly be generated. We will contact an environmental engineering company to advise us on any problems, as well as solutions, including legal disposal of all future wastes that may be identified. This owner believes in the "Green Philosophy" and will use recyclable and green products whenever possible.

We will also develop a relationship with local Food Pantries to donate our excess food items. We will also make additional donations for holiday functions such as Thanksgiving and Christmas dinners.

CUSTOMERS

There have been numerous sites identified where customers are located that would purchase our top-notch homemade BEST BBQ foods and drinks. During the cold weather, our downtown site will be opened and will become a popular location for our customers to continue to patronize because of its extremely busy location.

We will enhance these BBQ dishes with our special and secret family recipes that will attract numerous customers. It is projected that families who enjoy our unique BEST BBQ food lines and will eagerly come back for more.

MARKETING & ADVERTISEMENT

The image of BEST BBQ is to offer exciting, delicious and healthy food and drink items of the finest quality at a reasonable price. The market area will be surrounding communities. We will target the large number of people who come and seek good food in the summer months. When it turns cold, our downtown site will be ready and waiting for our customers.

We will build a web site and maintain an ongoing presence in the social media market place to attract our customers. Newspaper and radio advertisement will be researched along with a TV commercial.

"Word of Mouth" is a powerful advertisement tool and we will continue to promote this method by offering some type of reward when one of our customers recommends us.

Business cards will also be utilized in our ongoing advertisement efforts. We will join the Chamber of Commerce and attend all of their after hours business events where we will distribute our business cards and do heavy networking. We will also attend food trade shows to learn about new and innovative marketing and advertisement techniques.

During the first three months, $960 will be allocated and spent on advertisement strategies. From then on, 2% of sales will be set aside for advertisement, but only after we inquire from our customers how they heard about our company. These inquiries will determine the most effective advertisement and what we should continue with or cease. We will measure our advertisement effectiveness by asking all of our customers how they heard about BEST BBQ.

COMPETITORS

We do expect advances to be made and competitors to arise. We will meet these challenges by hiring additional staff and branching out into new sites.

We will add original new food items to keep our customers coming back for more. Let us state upfront that none of our competitors offer anything like our BEST BBQ foods, drinks and desserts.

#1 Competitor:

Name   Domino's Pizza Parlor (National Franchise)
Address   470 French Road
            City, State
Strengths:

        Location -   Location is good

                Pricing -   Low cost producer

                Delivery -   Delivers as promised

                Management - Everyone appears to be fully trained

Weaknesses:

	Service -	In-house service is slow
		Their product line is pizza only
	Overhead -	Lacks visible signage

#2 Competitor:

Name	Tony's Café
Address	8 Burrstone Road
	City, State

Strengths:

	Location -	An acceptable site and they deliver
	Pricing -	Known for aggressive pricing policy
	Delivery -	Delivery system is prompt
	Management -	Appear to be well trained

Weaknesses:

	Service -	Offer no healthy food choices
		There are no sitting accommodations
	Overhead -	Spends little on advertisement

#3 Competitors
:

Name	Nino's Pub
Address	234 Main St.
	City, State

Strengths:

	Location -	The parking is not a problem
	Pricing -	Low cost producer
	Delivery -	They do not cater but do deliver
	Management -	Management appears strong

Weaknesses:

	Service -	Takes too long to be served
		They do not offer any healthy food
	Overhead -	Spends very little on advertisement

We anticipate that new competitors will surface and substantially reproduce our results, but not to the degree of perfection that we have achieved. To remain on the leading edge, we will devote 2% of revenues toward research and development of new products to meet the emerging needs of our customers.

Due to the fast changing nature of any food industry, we will need to retrofit our methods of producing our BBQ food items each year. The owner, Morey Best, proposes to use "just good solid" business sense, economies of scale, and the use of efficient financial techniques.

ANTICIPATED FIXED MONTHLY EXPENSES

Downtown Monthly Lease	400
Utilities:	400
Telephone:	230
Book Keeping Services	150
Owner salary:	1,500
Employees:	3,000
Advertising:	300
Insurance:	200
TOTAL:	**$6,180**

INITIAL INVENTORY (ASSETS)

Food Containers & Lids	450
Utensils	360
Paper Products	625
Various Kinds of Drinks	500
Variety of Meats	850
Rolls & Bread	525
Pastries & A Variety of Desserts	320
Variety of Homemade Chips	390
TOTAL =	**$ 4,020**

LOAN RATIONALE

Mobile Truck fully equipped is $ 67,000

Down payment by Owner from his savings = $ 10,000

The sole owner, Morey Best, can make the monthly truck payments of $600 from his profits or from his saving account. Morey has an excellent credit rating of 763 and has no outstanding debts. The downtown site will be renovated and equipped at no cost to Morey.

This is a request for a line of credit of $36,000 to cover operating capital. This Business Action Plan is currently, being reviewed by Ms. Jane Jones the Loan Officer at XXX Bank.

ATTACHMENT 2

BUSINESS ACTION PLAN

THE STRONG FITNESS CENTER

Jules Strong, BSN, MS
Founder & CEO

10 Main Street
City, State
Tele: (890) 1234567

EXECUTIVE SUMMARY

The Strong Fitness Center Inc. was established as a corporation by Jules Strong who is the founder and sole owner. She has always had a vision of opening her own fitness center and has the credentials and expertise to successfully start-up this business. After extensive research in the fields of health, wellness and fitness, she determined that now is the time to open her own fitness facility.

Jules conducted intensive research and after targeted marketing strategies, she has a waiting list of over two hundred clients who want to join her Center as soon as "the doors open". She has determined that this number of enrollees will more than cover her operating costs and yield an acceptable profit margin to pay back any business loan. Jules is in the process of purchasing the building at 200 Main Street. Her financial advisor provided data that support the purchase of this building to ensure current and future growth. Her business attorney concurs with this purchase plan.

This facility is the only one in a thirty-mile radius that can accommodate our specific fitness services. There are four local gyms, but none of these offer the training at the level that we will, nor are these large enough to accommodate any future expansions. With the assistance from her financial advisor, Jules is seeking a business loan to purchase her facility and some additional funds to apply toward the equipment costs. The initial operating capital request will be assumed through a line of credit that will be paid back out of future projected profits. Her father operates a well established construction company and has agreed to complete $47,000 in renovations, at no cost to Jules.

According to the latest health magazines, fitness is growing in popularity across the Nation. This is to our advantage because we will be the only full-service health, wellness and fitness provider in this area. Jules is dedicated to providing a comprehensive training regime that makes numerous clients want to join. Additional potential clients are contacting us everyday and are put on the waiting list. They will commence their membership as soon as our new fully-equipped Center is opened.

The Strong Fitness Center Inc. was established with the goal of becoming a strong leader in the fitness arena that will focus on unique, functional and everyday physical movements. Specific programs are designed to get our clients in the best shape of their life, under the guidance of highly trained skilled coaches. Clients will not wander around the gym wondering what to do. We strive to help them improve their overall fitness with functional movement performed at high intensity, using a targeted variety of workouts. Our programs feature the sport of fitness which is a dynamic new approach to exercise that is turning the traditional gym activities "upside down".

COMPANY HISTORY

Jules Strong researched and formed this new company to bring quality fitness education and training to the various levels of our clients where state-of-the-art equipment will be used.

The main goal is to bring life-long fitness to the forefront of educational, health, wellness and fitness initiatives. Financing to purchase the building has just been finalized with the loan officer of XYZ Bank. Renovations are now underway and equipment has been ordered and will be arriving in two weeks.

We anticipate achieving higher levels of profitability in the first year of operations because of the above-average client membership. The rationale for the maximized increase profit level is that the amount of actual income will increase due to the high volume of our client base. After this building is purchased, renovated and new equipment is installed; we will have our Grand Opening.

Jules and her financial advisor researched all of the operating expenses that were anticipated and it was mathematically feasible to achieve profitability early on. The newly-created children's program will generate numerous kid enrollees because it's currently not available in this area.

The following business initiatives have been accomplished:

- The acceptable client membership quota has been exceeded
- Our Bank has reviewed our Plan and approved the loan
- This building has been purchased
- Three certified fitness instructors have been screened/hired
- Equipment has been ordered and will arrive in two weeks

The owner, Jules of The Strong Fitness Center Inc. believes very strongly in technical, financial, business and moral excellence. Our goal is to provide the finest health, wellness and fitness programs to our clients.

Jules is establishing a track record of creative ideas such as combining fitness education, healthy products and life-long learning techniques, thereby addressing the overall fitness value to our clients. More clients will purchase products and services because of our reasonable price scale, thus increasing our market share.

HISTORY OF HEALTH, WELLNESS & FITNESS

The first structured Fitness Center that was established as a formal business enterprise can be found as far back as the early 1900's. Exercise and fitness has always played a major role throughout the centuries.

Health-related activities including the basic fitness routines were very popular in the original concept until well into the 20th century when new and focused types of health, wellness and fitness techniques were introduced.

Fitness studios and similar companies have enjoyed a period of steady growth over the past twenty years. This demand is due to many factors, not the least of which is the advancement of new and innovative fitness activities.

At this time, there are only three local gyms that offer very restrictive services. The advantage of our company is that it will be the only one of its kind in this region that provides our members with an array of services targeting the holistic approach to wellness.

Jules has already developed an outstanding reputation in the fields of health, wellness and fitness training here in this area. All of our clients will undergo a personal strengths, weaknesses, opportunities and threats (SWOT) analysis. This is their individualized fitness-risk analysis to identify their needs. Only professionally-trained coaches will meet with each client to design a personalized program and follow them along the way. She will train her coaches to look at the "big picture" so that customers will keep coming back.

THE CURRENT MARKET PLACE

Recently, the XXX Insurance Company, City and State reported savings of $1.7 million dollars annually that was attributed to employee fitness programs. The XXX Company in City and State also cited in its recent year-end report, a savings of $1 million dollars per year by implementing employee fitness programs.

Currently, there are no corporate-sponsored fitness programs for employees in this immediate area. We have started to target major companies that are located in the surrounding region and have spoken to the top managers in six of these companies. They have agreed to consider our proposal to establish the Employee

Health/Wellness/Fitness Club membership for their employees. Three of these managers have already agreed to this membership proposal as soon as we open.

Jules will continue to meet and inform other company managers how their business can profit by enrolling employees in programs that are designed to increase fitness, decrease absenteeism and will benefit their "bottom profit line".

FUTURE KEY ASSUMPTIONS

1. A constantly growing economy without any major recession

2. No unpredictable changes in fitness or medical concerns

3. No major National or global events that threaten health issues

In addition, we will start conducting free Informational Seminars every Monday and Thursday evening from 7 to 8 pm to attract additional clients.

Advances will be made in the fields of health, wellness and fitness and new competitors will emerge that will try to offer similar products and services and these will be address by measuring our advertisement initiatives by the increase of membership and make investments in new fitness techniques and related equipment.

MANAGEMENT

Founder and Chief Executive Officer: Jules Strong

Jules is a Certified Fitness Instructor, Registered Dietitian and Nutritionalist who has an extensive background in healthy eating and fitness skills that she acquired at the local hospital and the University of City and State. She is a very effective community leader and has achieved numerous awards in her respective professional fields. Jules studied stress management, the impact of stress on the body and the specific skills needed to combat the negative effects of ongoing stress physically and mentally.

She is responsible for providing leadership, monitoring and control of all aspects of this operation, while working with her team of employees. She will use the team approach to effectively operate this business venture. Team efforts will contribute to the overall effective management strategies, aimed at performance excellence while serving our clients. This team came to the consensus that targeted marketing and advertisement strategies be implemented to ensure a sufficient membership count well before we open.

This owner of The Strong Fitness Center proposes to use good solid business sense by utilizing effective and efficient management techniques that will allow these options:

- Expand at our current site as client enrollment grows
- Increase the profit margin due to new children programs
- Conduct free weekly Informational Seminars
- Monitor our pricings to ensure an acceptable profit level
- Increase ongoing exposure to the public at large
- Become actively involved in community events

Manager: Mr. Rex Reed

Rex is extremely talented and experienced in the field of health management. Supervising a business is not new to Rex because he was employed as the manager of a local gym for ten years, but the owner retired and closed the business.

He brings not only the technical and fitness expertise, but strong management skills into the operations. He has over ten years in the fitness arena during which he developed the unique skills for effective healthy living and wellness through an effective fitness regime. His blend of specific technical and management skills will contribute to the success of this business.

Financial Advisor: Ms. Justine Miller

Justine Miller is a local book keeper who will work part time and be responsible for the financial activities of this company and will compile all of the necessary financial data. The company's financial accounts will be set up, monitored and maintained by Justine who will regularly discuss pertinent data with Jules.

A computerized accounting system will be installed to consistently monitor our financial performance. This information will be compiled at the end of each month for preparation of our financial statements. Overall costs witll be regularly evaluated to ensure that we are achieving the best possible fees. Justine will follow the financial standards set forth by Dunn & Bradstreet.

Marketing Executive: Mr. Mel Gifford

The Marketing Executive for this firm is Mel Gifford who is one of the top professionals of a local advertisement firm. He will be hired as the outside consultant to market and advertise this company.

Mel graduated in 2012 from the University of XXX, City and State, majoring in Advertisement and Marketing. His post graduate work was performed at the Sabine Institute in City and State where he published a current National research paper entitled "The Future of Global Marketing & Advertisement Strategies Impacting Small Business".

PROFESSIONAL STAFFING

Immediate staffing will include three trained professionals, one administrative assistant and Jules, the owner. Additional professionally trained coaches will be hired when the need arises and/or work on an appointment-driven basis. Critical aspects that were sought in employees are professionals who are client oriented, friendly, and fully trained.

Jules is a trained and certified professional fitness coach who will specifically oversee all of the team members. She is also working on the newly created Next Step Fitness for Kids program. This is a program to encourage children to do well in all of the things that they do best, such as, running, jumping, rolling, swinging, climbing, crawling, throwing balls and being "upside down".

In addition to the Center, there will be the Strong Library that will house health, wellness and fitness-related educational resources that participants can use. There will be a Health Bar that will feature healthy food items and drinks. The business ratios for this company indicate strong financial growth and an impressive chance for investment opportunities by these further expansions.

The Next Step Fitness Center's programs and servces will include:

- High-intensity expanded fitness site and running paths
- Private offices for conducting the clients' SWOT Surveys
- Specialty Courses such as Endurance, Goal Setting, Gymnastics, Kettlebells, Mobility, Oly Lifting, Power Lifting & Children's Programs
- Cardiovascular machines will include treadmills, stair steppers, exercise bikes and other essential equipment. Various strength-related machines that work legs, chest, back, arms and shoulders. Free weights ranging from 2 to 100 lbs and each station will include benches.
- There will also be a variety of miscellaneous equipment; medicine balls, ropes, bands, ab wheels, floor mats, and various health-related charts

Classes will be: aerobics, youth health boot camp, Pilate's, yoga and special sessions for professionals, youth and seniors.

The Health Bar will be open where clients can purchase protein drinks, protein bars, juices and healthy light snacks. The Strong Library will be open for relaxing and learning about new fitness literature and concepts. Many clients said that they would welcome a short break to relax with a book and a drink before resuming their session.

This owner started with prior research on the subjects of life-long health, wellness and fitness and how this could best be achieved. This idea was reinforce by her study of additional fitness methods and programs.

Our coaches will strive to assist clients to find their own inner motivation in the areas of health, wellness and fitness and these professionals monitor their ongoing activities. The strengths of this company and the ability to grow are:

- Affordable client membership fees
- Qualified coaches and other team members
- Running paths during the nice weather
- State-of-the-art equipment
- In a safe and clean facility

We will commence by identifying our clients strengths, weaknesses, opportunities for fitness and threats though the SWOT Survey in order to kick off their life-long well being activities. Their personalized Plan of action is based upon the findings in their survey. Their Plan will be implemented, then reviewed periodically and modified on a regular basis, under the guidance of our trained coaches.

The Strong Fitness Center was created to address these market conditions:

- Start-up and growth opportunities for a full-service and focused Fitness Center exist in the fields of health, wellness and fitness
- Our records show that there are 177 individuals who will join as soon as we open the doors
- There are many other prospective individuals who have expressed serious interest in becoming clients

The desire and confidence to take this business to the next level will be to implement the plan of action, thereby increasing the client-base and ultimately the overall profit margin.

By seeking the professional experience and expertise at the Entrepreneur Center, this owner will bring this business to a successful fruition. This owner has the knowledge, expertise, and enthusiasm that make clients come here for help with the fitness concepts that affect their lives forever. Motivation of others is what Jules does best!

FINANCIAL PLANNING

In order to maintain a level of long range financial security for The Strong Fitness Center, monitoring by our financial manager will be an integral segment of this operation.

A healthy and secure financial future for this company is critical to its ongoing success, as denoted by being aware of the overhead costs of overhead, salaries and other costs that impact the budget. Salaries and loan payments are two major expenses that will be very closely monitored.

CLIENT PROFILE

There are numerous potential clients of all ages who are interested in becoming healthy, fit and well, but just need the motivational team to bring this to fruition for their well being by joining our program.

Clients will learn the art of healthy exercising with a purpose, daily mental activities, how to manage stress and the art of succeeding. These activities all focus on the individual member's life long plan of fitness. A member who needs specific agility training will enroll in specific activities to supplement their long-range fitness Plan and also consider taking health-related supplements. Professional adults and children who are interested in health, wellness, healthy living and fitness or just for fitness recreation will join our Center.

Some clients may want to achieve different levels of fitness and will join our special groups throughout the year where they can learn specific fitness techniques. "Kid Fitness" Programs that will be underway, will accommodate a great many children who will be trained under the guidance of certified professionals who have accreditation in the pediatric fitness field.

We will offer free weekly Informational Seminars to attract new clients by helping them to realize the importance of healthy living. Clients can also go to The Strong Library where they will find the latest fitness educational and other fact finding resources to reinforce their need to stay fit.

At a later time, when we have settled in to our facilities, local companies will be targeted to consider our Corporate Fitness Program because these employers will come to realize the importance of healthy employees through our one-on-one meetings.

PRODUCT & SERVICE DESCRIPTION

The owner of The Strong Fitness Center Inc. intends to offer the finest quality of health, wellness and fitness products and services through functional group fitness classes. Currently, these classes range in size of up to 25, depending on the attendance for that day and the enrollment at any given time.

When we originally thought of opening this business, class size was considered to be 10 to 12, but research shows that these client numbers could expand to 24, with no problems and would generate additional profits.

We will add new and emerging health and fitness related products to our Health Bar and Shoppe, as we continue to grow. The special products in the Health Shoppe will be made available to both clients and other patrons because it features specific vitamins, health products, healthy teas, coffee and health drinks not sold anywhere else in this area.

In addition, we will promote our business by selling apparel with The Strong Fitness Center name and logo on each piece.

To remain on the leading edge of quality fitness education, we will need to devote approximately 05% of revenues toward research and development of new services and techniques that will complement our current programs.

Due to the fast changing nature of the fitness industry, we will need to retrofit these techniques within two years. In order to address any seasonal fluctuations that may occur, we will offer new and exciting activities, such as the Kids Summer Fitness Camp and the newly created Outside Fitness Series during the nice weather.

Client research data reveal that in the winter months our enrollment will increase because our Center is the only one in this immediate area that offers reasonable fees all winter long.

PRICING

Pricing is established by the ongoing awareness of the owner who researched the current allowances in the existing market place. At this time, our major services are comparable to other gyms. This signifies that it will allow for an ongoing healthy profit margin for The Strong Fitness Center.

By the owner's continuous research in the area of pricing, we will achieve higher sales at the existing prices. As a result of increased sales, we will achieve higher return on investment (ROI) levels in the delivery of services to our clients. Through these economies of scale, many of our services can be rendered at reasonable prices that will yield higher net profits.

PRICING OUR SERVICES:

Pricing will be according to standard methods allowing for a profit, yet still remaining competitive. Clients will be continuously polled as to their wants and needs and then our service lines will change according to these responses.

Before we set the fee for each service, we will forecast what our fixed monthly costs are going to be. We will then determine what the market rate for comparable services are and at this rate we will determine that for all but the lowest billing projections, this specific service would turn a profit at a known rate. Since our services are quite unique and demand a higher level of expertise, we decided that we should bill slightly above our competitors.

PRICING OUR PRODUCTS:

Initially, we will set the prices for our health products, utilizing an "a unit basis" of what the costs are going to be. Then we will determine what the market price is for each item. At this price it will be determined that for all but the lowest sales projections our products will turn a profit at this given price.

It is predicted that since our health products are unique, we could price it according to items in the "real world". To test this price, we will poll a database of twenty of our clients. We will first question them about the desirability of a specific product and then asked them if the price of this product is acceptable. If a product is not to our clients' liking or the cost is not acceptable, then it will be eliminated.

MARKETING & ADVERTISEMENT

The image of The Strong Fitness Center is to offer the finest and most effective leading edge fitness services at a reasonable, customary and prevailing charge. Currently, our company is featured on Face book and has over 800 hits per day. Over 75% of our new clients are referrals or have seen our image on Face book.

Once our site is fully equipped, there will be a Grand Opening and will have massive media and television exposure, with numerous Gift Certificates and other promotional items. Then the use of several marketing Medias will be implemented to further promote our business such as we will:

- Continue to maintain a "first-rate" web site that is visible on numerous social media marketing sites where we will feature the owner and personnel profiles, hours of operation, membership rates, information about special classes and other activities
- Contact business owners and managers to offer discounted rates to their company as a whole or to their employees as part of their "employee benefits" package
- Sell retail health products, t-shirts, sweat shirts, hoodies, tank tops, shorts, etc, featuring the Next Step Fitness Center Inc. branding and logo
- Post details on our web site of upcoming events

In addition, we will research the use of Bill Boards as an effective method of long lasting advertisement strategies. "Word of Mouth" is a powerful advertisement tool and we will continue to promote this method by offering some type of reward to our faithful clients who recommend our products and services to others who join.

Business cards will also be utilized in our ongoing advertisement efforts. Direct contact in all of the regional Fitness and Health Trade Shows is a "must" in order to attract new clients.

We will consider a television commercial once we have established our business and after we have consulted with a marketing and advertisement firm as to the related costs.

Another marketing and advertisement initiative will be our own news letter that will be developed in-house and posted on the Internet. It will include all upcoming events that clients can get involved in. We will include the latest in health, wellness and fitness news.

During the first three months, approximately $1,000 per month will be spent on aggressive advertisement strategies. From then on, 5% of sales will be set aside for advertisement. We will continuously measure our advertisement effectiveness by specifically asking all current and prospective clients how they heard about The Strong Fitness Center and then adjust our advertisement strategies according to the responses by our clients.

COMPETITORS

Let us state up front that there are no other extensive facilities like ours operating within a one hundred mile radius. There are some limited competitors, but none of these offer what we provide our clients. In addition, we have researched the services of over eighty per cent of these possible competitors and there were none found that offered the specific line of full services that our company does.

There are several gyms currently operating in this area and these facilities focus primarily on exercise, with little emphasis on personalizing Plans for its clients and this makes our company a "cut above" all the others. Our facility is not just a fitness club, as the majority of our competitors are. Our company is in the business of long-term fitness management.

Our major function is to work with our clients to implement life-long individualized fitness activities. Unlike our competitors, we have a personal vested interest whereby we establish a partnership with all of our clients so that they achieve their own personalized goals.

Competitor #1

Name	*The Fitness Mill*
	City, State

Strengths:

Location - Site is average,

Owner present and very friendly
Pricing was average

Weaknesses:

Service - No life-long fitness Plans
Staff lack structured methods

Personnel are new & untrained

Competitor #2

Name	*Next Level Fitness*
	City, State

Strengths:

Location - An established name

Site - In a good location

Weaknesses:

Service - Pricing is very high

No life-long fitness Plans for its clients

No outside activities available
Management appears rude to clients
Employees lack basic fitness skills

Competitor #3

Name	*All-Fitness Center*
	City, State

Strengths:

> **Location - Site is in a good location**
>
> **Membership costs are low**

Weaknesses:

> **Service - No life-long fitness plans**
>
> **Appears to be the place to just "hang out"**
>
> **Very little parking available**
>
> **Employees lack direction**
>
> **Staff appears to have little formal training**

OUR COMPETITIVE ADVANTAGES

The distinctive competitive advantage that we bring into this market place is one-of-a-kind training not offered anywhere else in this area. There is over twenty years of professional team experience.

We have a structured finance plan that results in our being the low-cost provider in these price-sensitive markets and pricing will include a financial benefit to our long-term clients.

Our overhead will be kept reasonable through ongoing monitoring so that profits can be funneled back into the operation, thus avoiding high debt ratios.

GROWTH STRATEGIES

A new corporate business program will be implemented at our Center because the state of America's health care, coupled with vast demographic changes threatens to not only exacerbate the fitness crisis, but further erode employee productivity as well. The current corporate assumption all over the Nation is based on the belief that employees who are more fit are happier and more efficient.

Our corporate program will render fitness services that will help employees achieve the greatest gift of all; their good health. This program will potentially lead to decreased employee health care costs due to the reduction of: absenteeism, worker compensation costs, shorter hospital stays and lower insurance premiums. The time is right for us to go into action!

ANTICIPATED FIXED MONTHLY EXPENSES

Loan Repayment	$	1,000
Telephone & Internet		170
Employee Wages		6,400
Owner's Salary		2,000
Employee Compensation/Taxes		1,000
Book keeping Services		200
Insurance		750
Marketing & Advertisement		500
Postage/Mailings		165
Cleaning/Maintenance		160

TOTAL = $ 12,345

LOAN RATIONALE

Jules, the owner of Strong Fitness Center, has a current credit rating of 800 and has no outstanding debts.

She will use $50,000 of her savings toward the purchase of $100,000 new equipment and is requesting a loan for the remaining $50,000.

In addition, she is requesting $190,000 to purchase the facility. The total loan request is $240,000.

The XYZ Bank has already agreed to hold the mortgage as the loan guarantee.

Renovations estimated at $38,000 will be completed in two weeks by skilled family members, at no cost to Jules.

ABOUT THE AUTHOR

Dr. Patricia Laino, the author, is truly a remarkable businesswoman who achieved the American Dream. She gained success by overcoming poverty, attaining an education and working hard at starting her own business.

She lived it, did it and she teaches it! Her friends, colleagues and entrepreneur students call her Dr. Pat.

A few of Dr. Pat's awards are: Woman Advocate of the Year by the Federal Small Business Administration, Outstanding Alumni by the State University of New York and the Metropolitan Business & Professional Woman of the Year Award.

GLOSSARY

ACCOUNTS PAYABLE: A list of current debts or liabilities of a company

ACCOUNTS RECEIVABLE: A list of the amounts a firm is owed by others for merchandise or services sold, representing current assets

ANGEL INVESTORS: These are similar to Venture Capitalists. They loan money and take a risk of getting a high degree of profit on their investment

ASSETS: Cash or other items that will normally be turned into cash

BALANCE SHEET: A detailed listing of assets, liabilities and owner's equity accounts denoting the company's financial position

BREAK EVEN ANALYSIS: The level of sales at which your total sales covers your total costs and operating expenses

BURNOUT: Long term stress that if left unresolved will result

CAPITAL: Funds which are needed for the base of the business

CASH FLOW: The actual movement of cash within a business

COLLATERAL: Property pledged by a borrower to secure a loan

COPY RIGHT: Protection for an original work of authorship

CURRENT LIABILITIES: Amount owed

CURRENT RATIO: A ratio of a firm's current assets to its liabilities

DBA: "Doing Business As" filed by sole proprietors

EQUITY: Equity is the owner's investment in the business. Unlike capital, equity is what remains after the liabilities are subtracted

EQUITY FUNDS: You sell an interest in your business and you give a part of the profits to an investor

FIXED ASSETS: Those items required for the normal conduct of business and not converted into cash during a normal fiscal year

GROSS PROFITS: Net sales (sales minus returned merchandise, discounts or other allowances) minus the costs of goods sold

GUARANTY: Pledge by a third party to repay a loan if the borrower cannot

INCOME STATEMENT: Statement of income and expenses for a given period

LONG TERM CREDIT: Loans for more than a year commonly used for buying equipment, renovations or expansions

NET WORTH: Owner's equity is represented by the excess of total assets over total amount owed to outside creditors at a given time

NOTE: A note represents a loan which will be repaid, usually within a short period of time at a stated interest rate

PRO FORMA: Projections of what may result in the future from actions now

RATES-VARIABLES: Variable loan rates will change monthly or quarterly and be based on some index such as the bank's prime rate

SMALL BUSINESS ADMINISTRATION (SBA): SBA does not give loans but give loan dollars to acceptable Banks and they do the loan

SECURED LOAN: A loan protected by owner's collateral

SHORT TERM CREDIT: Banks and other lenders will loan you money to purchase inventory for special reasons (holidays)

TERM LOAN: Either secured or unsecured loan for periods of more than one year and are paid off similar to a mortgage

TRADE CREDIT: This is the money owed to a supplier who permits you to have an open account called "buying on credit"

VENTURE CAPITAL FIRMS: The difference between a Venture Capitalist (VC) and a Bank is: Banks are creditors that look for a steady flow of repayments. VCs are stock owners who take more of a risk and expect profits

WORKING CAPITAL: The difference between current assets and current liabilities